LET GO &
RUN BESIDE

"What you'll find in this book are practical lessons that are tried and true. They have been tested with and experienced by preteens over the past fifteen years. Sean and the team at *FourFiveSix.org* have developed a strategy of ministry that intentionally reaches preteens and helps them connect to Jesus. This is THE BOOK on preteen ministry."

—Patrick Snow, VP of Content, Christ In Youth,
Creator of SuperStart! Preteen Conferences

"Intentional Preteen Ministry should be a bright spot in your church. This book will show you how to make it happen. I'm thankful for Sean Sweet. His commitment to serving preteens at his local church and preteen ministries around the globe is phenomenal. I wish I'd had this book when I started in children's ministry!"

—Ryan Frank, CEO/Publisher at KidzMatter

"There is a life-defining window of development that opens during the preteen years, and within this window, you'll find one of life's most powerful kingdom-building opportunities. This opportunity is certainly redeemable if missed because that is how God rolls. But...we don't have to miss it. Focus and intentionality go a long way and the principles of *Let Go & Run Beside* will help you to seize this opportunity to the max!"

—Paula Mazza, Director of Children's & Preteen Ministries, Solana
Beach Pres, CA, Founder of *PreteenMentalHealth.com*

"People never plan to have an accident. Accidents happen on their own. Effective ministry doesn't work that way. It takes prayer, it takes planning, it takes intentionality. The Intentional Preteen Ministry strategies Sean Sweet has explained in this book will help you, your workers, and your preteens prepare for all the "accidents" that come up as children move through the challenges of early adolescence and take their first steps of faith ownership."

—James Powell, Director of Preteens, Brooklyn Tabernacle, NY

"This timely (yet timeless) message from Sean is a clear and powerful invitation to champion the discipleship of preteens. You won't just be inspired to reach preteens more effectively—you will actually be equipped to take a step forward in a ministry to preteens that has tremendous Kingdom impact. Sean is a trustworthy guide for preteen ministry leaders, and he has given us a great gift in this book. Read it to see what I mean."

—Michayla White, Executive Director, International Network of Children's Ministry

"WOW! This was inspiring to read. It was an encouraging reminder of why we do what we do with preteens. I have gotten to enjoy the benefits of Intentional Preteen Ministry, as a preteen and now as an adult leader in a ministry designed around the principles of this book."

—Makenna Shrum, Preteen Ministry Assistant (and former preteen), Destiny Christian Church, CA

"Please buy this book. My husband worked hard on it."

—Dayna Sweet, Sean's wife and partner in ministry

THE ESSENTIALS OF INTENTIONAL PRETEEN MINISTRY

LET GO & RUN BESIDE

BY SEAN SWEET

FourFiveSix
Raising the value of your ministry to preteens

FO
UR

HOLD UP!

Before you start reading this book, get
the most out of your experience!

Check out all the resources at:
LetGoAndRunBeside.com

WHAT IS INTENTIONAL PRETEEN MINISTRY?

An Intentional Preteen Ministry is one in which leaders understand the unique needs and developmental characteristics of preteens, and in which leaders are actively creating experiences that facilitate preteens' movement into faith ownership.

If we're going to help 9- to 12-year-olds develop meaningful personal relationships with Jesus, we desperately need an intentionally-designed ministry where leaders use proven strategies that work for the difficult, wacky, unique, exciting, God-designed stage known as the preteen years.

This book will give you ten of those strategies: ten essentials of Intentional Preteen Ministry.

ACKNOWLEDGEMENTS

My name is on the cover, but the ideas and discoveries in this book aren't mine alone. They belong to amazing leaders from all over who've walked beside me as we've learned together what Intentional Preteen Ministry is. At retreats, conferences, and online meetings, many of the ideas in the book were formulated; but most of the time, I couldn't tell you who had the idea first and who added to it. Sometimes, it's hard for me to know where one person's idea ends and somebody else's idea begins.

In short, this book was a team effort. Here, then, are the names of the Four-FiveSix leadership team, both former and current. These are my co-laborers in the development of this idea called Intentional Preteen Ministry:

Patrick Snow, Heather Dunn, Nick Diliberto, Jim Keat, Nate Cummings, Mike Sheley, Rob Tuma, Mike Branton, Katie Gerber, Chip Henderson, Rob Quinn, Paula Mazza, and James Powell.

I also am eternally grateful to Pastor Greg Fairrington. He has been an amazing pastor and boss. He helped lead me to the Lord, he performed my wedding, and he has given me incredible opportunities in ministry! He has sought not only to understand my vision and calling but also to support it in ways that go beyond what I ever would have expected from anybody. He has led our local church in giving the support needed for the Intentional Preteen Ministry movement to take flight around the world. Pastor Greg is a local pastor with global impact, and I am thankful to God for him!

In the trenches of ministry, there has been nobody (besides my wife) I've enjoyed working with more than Chris Santos. I learned so much by working with my good friend over decades of ministry together, and we both challenged each other to grow. Many of the ideas in this book were birthed out of conversations (and the occasional argument) with my buddy, Chris.

Many thanks to Mark Campbell for continuing to help Intentional Preteen Ministry grow from a great idea into a movement.

My family has been extremely supportive in a million ways all along. My parents, Roger and Carol Sweet, gave me a great foundation on which to build a life and a ministry. My wife, Dayna Sweet, and my children, Serene, Savannah, and Daniel, have been such an amazing blessing and have brought me so much joy through the years. My family has given me such a great gift; they've allowed and encouraged me to pursue God's calling on my life.

There have been so many wonderful co-laborers in ministry through the years who've added to my understanding and my joy in ministry, and I really hope they won't feel slighted that I didn't mention their names here. The list is long, and each of you has contributed in amazing ways to my growth and fulfillment as a ministry leader. I am eternally grateful to God for each of you.

—Sean

WARNING

If you're looking for strategies to make preteens "behave," you've picked up the wrong book. If you're looking for techniques to help you manipulate preteens into accepting what you're teaching as The Truth, you should stop reading this book right now.

If, however, you're looking for ways to create space for preteens to move toward:

- a faith in God that is THEIRS,
- a love of God's Word that is THEIRS, and
- a walk with Jesus Christ that is THEIRS,

and if you're looking for ways to encourage and love preteens during this sometimes difficult process, **then you are I are on the same page, and I can't wait to go on this journey with you!**

In this book, we're going to dive into ten essentials that will help preteens move into a faith that's all their own. The chapters aren't meant to be an exhaustive list of effective techniques for helping preteens to "own it," but rather a collection of ten strategies that have proven highly effective over the years for ministry leaders in the FourFiveSix community.

Intentional Preteen Ministry starts with the willingness of caring leaders to let go and run beside, cheering on preteens as they take some of their first steps into faith ownership.

If you're ready to do that, then let's go! This is going to be exciting—it might even be life-changing!

CONTENTS

FOREWORD

One afternoon, inside a small cabin nestled in the middle of the Colorado Rockies, a group of preteen pastors from different churches engaged in a conversation about preteens. They discussed this question: "Is an intentional ministry to preteens important? Why or why not?"

An answer to a question as important as "Why preteen ministry?" doesn't happen in one sitting. It comes from years of commitment, passion, experience and, most importantly, listening to the Spirit of God. Eventually, an answer did emerge for this group in a moment of great clarity.

I had the privilege of being part of that initial discussion and the fruit that followed. Sean Sweet was there, too. In many ways, Sean is the beating heart that has kept alive the vision that emerged from those discussions since that moment of clarity in the Colorado Rockies over a decade ago. To this day, Sean has continued to advance the preteen ministry philosophy, and the national ministry to preteen leaders, that followed.

So, what answer emerged? What philosophy am I referring to? That's what this book is all about. The answers to this question, and a whole lot more, are what you'll find throughout these pages. Sean has done a beautiful job capturing the "Aha!" moments and lessons learned throughout the journey launched by our initial discussion.

If you're like me, the type of knowledge you desire to gain comes from more than just statistical analysis. You want the knowledge and wisdom that only comes from the front lines of ministry—from folks who have served in the trenches and have lived to tell about it. That's what you'll get from Sean. He's a veteran preteen pastor who's ministered to and served 4th, 5th, and 6th grade students for over two decades. His passion for preteens—that they understand, and be followers of, Christ—has been the defining purpose of his life, and it lives on every page of this book.

The lessons in this book come directly from practical, hands-on preteen ministry experiences. If it's in this book, I can assure you that it's been tried, tested, and refined by Sean or another passionate preteen pastor that he gleaned from along the way. These ideas WORK! Trust me. For almost two decades, I've been blessed to be a part of my own intentional ministry to preteens. Much of what's in this book has been implemented in that ministry. These concepts have produced understanding for the journey, as well as many joy-filled moments of seeing preteens connect with their Savior. Give the concepts here a shot. I'm confident that they'll do the same for your ministry, too.

Intentional Preteen Ministry is difficult to define, challenging to place, and in a constant state of change. It has a difficult time finding faithful leaders who are passionate about investing their time, energy, and CAREERS to see it become fruitful. I pray that, as you're reading this book, YOU will begin to see yourself as one of those faithful leaders.

As you will soon discover, preteens are at the unique stage of life in which they are taking their first steps into ownership. This includes owning their faith in Christ for the first time. Ministries and ministry leaders dedicated to helping them successfully do this are few and far between. There are some out there, including Sean and the FourFiveSix ministry...but they aren't enough.

Preteens needs more: more ministries faithful to coaching them; more researchers dedicated to discovering who they are; more leaders committed to letting go and running beside them.

This is your invitation. Come be a part of the movement.
Okay, that's it! On to what you came here for.

—Patrick Snow, VP of Content, Christ In Youth,
Creator of SuperStart! Preteen Conferences

ESSENTIAL 1: LET GO

Eleven-year-old Savannah bounds into our preteen ministry with a big smile on her face. She's always upbeat, but lately she has a contagious glow of happiness around her. That's because she's planning her twelfth birthday party.

Want to hear the idea she has for her party? Get ready; it's a doozy.

Step 1: Before the party, she'll ask each of her close friends what their LEAST favorite game is, and why they don't like it. *For example, Besty Brianna's least favorite game is soccer. Why? Because nobody passes the ball to her.*

Step 2: At the party, Savannah will lead her friends in playing everybody's least favorite game, but she'll change the rules to fix the "problems." *For example, they'll play soccer, but the new rule is that you must pass to Brianna.*

When Savannah shared her idea with us, my wife, who serves with me in our 4th-6th grade ministry, shot me a sideways glance. We both cracked half-smiles.

Is this a great idea for a birthday party? I'm leaning toward "no." This might even be a gigantic crash-and-burn experience for Savannah. Like so many of the ideas preteens cook up, this is a birthday party plan that's unlike anything I've ever experienced—and therefore, it's difficult for me to imagine that it will be successful. I think of the failed experiments I've had in my life, and a part of me wants to protect Savannah from experiencing those yucky feelings of failure.

The ideas of early adolescents come from a place of limited experience. Sometimes, these ideas fly in face of everything that seems wise. As we lead preteens, we can find ourselves scratching our heads as we wonder, "Why on earth would you do *that*?"

Preteens like Savannah are in a fragile point in their development. On one hand, they don't have the life experience necessary to make solid decisions. On the other hand, they're enthusiastic about making their own decisions.

So, how do we respond? How do we interface with preteens as they assume ownership of their lives, make plenty of obvious mistakes, and take unnecessary risks along the way?

IT MIGHT HELP TO CONSIDER THIS:

When a baby is born, he's not developmentally ready to walk. One day, he reaches an age where he is...except that he's not, because he's never done it before. *He's ready developmentally, but not experientially.*

This is when we encourage the baby to walk. We hold his hands and walk with him up and down the hallway countless times. One day, he scoots over to a coffee table on his own volition. He slowly stands, with pudgy fingers clinging tightly to the table and legs, struggling to find balance. Eventually, after a few wobbly moments, he lets go. He takes a few tentative steps and falls.

Now, think about what we do when he falls. Do we shake our heads disapprovingly and say, "What is *wrong* with you? Why are you acting like that?" Do we rescue him and insist that he not *ever* try walking again without our help? No. Of course not. We celebrate the steps forward with claps and encouraging words. We celebrate that he's slowly becoming a child who can walk on his own. This baby, who was once unable to walk, is now ready (developmentally, not experientially). We celebrate his experiments. We celebrate his efforts and his risk-taking. We encourage these things, because we know he needs these experiences to eventually stop falling and start walking with confidence.

Preteens, much like toddlers, are developmentally ready to use new functions, but they don't have the experience to know how to use these functions well. Many of us find it harder to respond with claps and encouraging words to preteens as they take risks because they aren't just taking stumbling steps and falling on the carpet. Instead, we see them:

- challenging what we're telling them about God
- crossing their arms and leaning against a wall during worship, with their friends then following suit
- distracting people around them while we're trying to communicate important truths
- making obviously bad choices without being able to explain why
- defending those obviously bad choices, against all reason and authority
- making obnoxious noises when it's clearly time to calm down

Cheering on a baby who is learning to walk comes much more naturally to most people; but what would it look like to cheer on a preteen?

WHEN DISCIPLING PRETEENS, I'VE HAD TO LEARN NOT TO GET UPSET AS THEY EXPLORE THEIR NEW CAPABILITIES.

This is easier when I consider what it's like to be a preteen. The mother of a sixth grader said something to me once, and I'll never forget it: *"As difficult as you may find it to be around preteens, it's often more difficult to be a preteen."*

Here's an equation I find useful when observing preteen behavior:

    LACK OF EXPERIENCE
+ DESIRE TO TRY NEW ABILITIES
+ DISCONCERTING FEELINGS ASSOCIATED WITH CHANGE
+ THE EMOTIONAL ROLLER COASTER OF HORMONES
─────────────────────────────────
PRETEEN BEHAVIOR

Preteens wake up as a slightly different version of themselves every day. According to the Association for Middle Level Education's (AMLE) comprehensive research article *Developmental Characteristics of Young Adolescents*, "In early adolescence [10-15 years old], the young adolescent body undergoes more developmental change than at any other time except from birth to two years old."[1]

Wow! That's an incredible amount of change in a short amount of time. We see this rapid change in the preteens who come to our church, don't we?

The change isn't just physical. Preteens are gaining new mental abilities on an almost weekly basis. Like a baby who discovers her feet for the first time, preteens are driven to explore their new abilities; and, just like a baby learning to walk or a kid learning to ride a bike, a preteen is going to make a lot of mistakes as he or she tries out these new abilities.

PRETEENS ARE SO CREATIVE.

Even though I have over twenty-five years of experience working with 4th-6th graders, I'm still surprised by ideas like Savannah's birthday party plan.

1   Caskey, Micki and Anfara, Jr., Vincent A. "Developmental Characteristics of Young Adolescents." Association for Middle Level Education. Published October 2014. https://www.amle.org/BrowsebyTopic/WhatsNew/WNDet/TabId/270/ArtMID/888/ArticleID/455/Developmental-Characteristics-of-Young-Adolescents.aspx.

I say they're "creative." Other people say "ridiculous," "dangerous," or even "downright stupid."

However, pressing against boundaries and thinking outside of the box is part of healthy development for a preteen. According to Abigail A. Baird, Professor of Psychological Science on the Arnhold Family Chair at Vassar College, "In the tween years, in the very beginning of adolescence, the world's yours. The possibilities are infinite...It might look like they're being self-centered on the surface, but [preteens are] actually being hyper-vigilant, they're being aware of themselves in context...which is a really important part of learning about the world. [Preteens] have to consider the possibilities."

Preteens exhibit many new behaviors because of developmental changes in the brain. The early adolescent brain is developing a plethora of functions that give 4th-6th graders "superpowers" they didn't have before. They're experiencing exponential changes in the ways they think and process information. They can begin to test hypotheses, think abstractly, and contemplate complex, unanswerable questions like never before. The AMLE article points out, "Intellectual development refers to the increased ability of people to understand and reason. In young adolescents, intellectual development is not as visible as physical development, but it is just as intense." Simple answers from the adults they trust no longer satisfy a preteen's curiosities: "Young adolescents often pose broad, unanswerable questions about life and refuse to accept trivial responses from adults."[2]

It's not just that preteens are thinking about different THINGS than younger kids; they are thinking in different WAYS—ways in which they could not think when they were younger.

It's not just birthday parties they're thinking about in new ways, either. It's everything—from their relationships with parents and pastors to their tastes in music. For the first time, they are developmentally able to take ownership of what they think and how they live. This is true in every aspect of their lives,

2   Ibid.

including how they think about God, the Church, and Christianity. For the first time, they are starting to lay *their own* foundation for the adult they will become.

An Intentional Preteen Ministry is one in which leaders understand the unique needs and developmental characteristics of preteens, and in which leaders are actively creating experiences that facilitate preteens' movement into faith ownership.

If we're going to help 9- to 12-year-olds develop meaningful personal relationships with Jesus, we desperately need an intentionally-designed ministry where leaders use proven strategies that work for the difficult, wacky, unique, exciting, God-designed stage known as the preteen years.

In early elementary ministries, children need a strong spiritual foundation to be poured for them. They need great examples and solid Biblical teaching so they can understand what faith in Christ looks like in action, and even so they can get some practical experience imitating a life of faith.

But preteens are ready to go beyond this. They're ready to start taking ownership of their walk with Jesus. To help them, we leaders must learn how to "let go of the bike."

HAVE YOU EVER TAUGHT SOMEBODY TO RIDE A BIKE?

I can still remember running up and down our street with my youngest daughter, one hand firmly on the back of the bicycle seat and the other hand on the handlebars. I taught her about balance. I taught her about steering. I taught her about making the pedals and brakes work. I did all this while holding on. But there came a day when it was time for me to let go. I'm not sure if she knew it first, or if I knew it, but it was clear that the day had arrived.

My daughter had zero experience riding a bike on her own. So experientially, she wasn't prepared. But developmentally, she was ready.

She was ready, but not ready.

Likewise, preteens are ready for us to "let go of the bike." They have new mental abilities—abilities that allow them to connect with Jesus in new and meaningful ways; but we must make room for them to do this.

This means that they will make mistakes. Still, we must "let go."

Patrick Snow of Christ In Youth explains what *letting go of the bike* in pre-teen ministry looks like:

- Helping preteens understand how to learn from the Bible themselves instead of just teaching them.
- Allowing them to discover how their faith affects their life instead of simply telling them.
- Inviting them to voice their own questions and answers about God, Jesus, and the Bible instead of just giving them ours.
- Creating opportunities for them to figure out on their own what God is calling them to do as servants in His Kingdom.

A GREAT EXAMPLE OF "LETTING GO OF THE BIKE" IS FOUND IN 1 SAMUEL CHAPTER 3.

Reread this familiar story with an eye on how Eli disciples Samuel when he receives a calling from the Lord. Samuel grew up "in church," and yet 1 Samuel 3:7 says that he did not know the Lord. How is that possible? Samuel grew up in the temple— he'd probably heard truths about God every day of his life. He even served in the temple! Still, Samuel had to have a first-hand, personal encounter with the Lord to really know him for himself, and one day, he was finally ready for this.

Picture the scene: It was the third time Samuel had walked to Eli's bedside that night, and Eli finally realized that God was calling Samuel.

How would you respond if you were Eli?

- "Why are you acting like this? I told you I didn't call you. Have you got a listening problem, kid? Go to your bedroom and don't bother me again!"
- "Okay, Samuel. That's God calling you. This is a big deal! I don't want you to mess this up, so I'm going to sit with you in your room. I know how to hear from God (I've been doing it for years), so I'll do it for you."

Eli didn't say either of these things. Instead, he "perceived that the Lord was calling the boy: "Therefore Eli said to Samuel, 'Go, lie down, and if he calls you, you shall say, "Speak, LORD, for your servant hears"'" (1 Samuel 3:8b-9). Eli let go of the bike. He made room for Samuel to have his own personal encounter with God.

Here was the result: Samuel went from not knowing the Lord (verse 7) to this: "Samuel grew, and the Lord was with him and let none of his words fall to the ground (verse 19)."

For most younger kids, we disciple well by showing them who God is and helping them know ABOUT God. But preteens are ready for more. Most are ready, developmentally, to take their first steps from knowing ABOUT God to knowing God for themselves.

That's a profound step, and even though most preteens are ready for this step developmentally, they—like Samuel—aren't ready experientially.

WE NEED TO BE WILLING TO LET GO.

Understanding why preteens are the way they are is a great first step; but if we care about the spiritual development of the preteens in our churches, we need to go way beyond simply tolerating and understanding them. Instead of just putting up with all the quirky, snarky, difficult behaviors preteens exhibit, what if we intentionally created ministry spaces to facilitate experimentation with their higher-level, never-before-tried cognitive abilities—in such a way that we lead them into having their own deep and personal relationships with Jesus?

If a preteen walked into your ministry with wings that had just grown out of his shoulder blades that morning, you could say, "Put those things away. There's no room for your wings here. If you try to flap them, you might hit a person or a wall, and the wind might mess up my neatly-stacked papers. Listen to me: if you flap those wings, you won't be allowed back, and I'll talk to your parents about clipping them. Understand?"

OR you could take an entirely different approach:

"Wow! Those are new! How great is this?! I totally believe you can use those wings to bring glory to God. In fact, we've created this place for you to try those wings out. Learning how to use those wings might be tricky, especially at first. That's okay. You'll figure this out, and we'll be right there when you need some help."

Preteens walk into our churches each week with invisible "wings." What will we do when they're ready to try them out?

- They have a new ability to reject what adults say and discover their own answers. *Are we going to stifle that or make room for it?*

- They appreciate more sophisticated levels of humor. *Are we going to stifle that or make room for it?*
- They have the ability to wrestle with their own moral choices. *Are we going to stifle that or make room for it?*
- They have a new desire for independence and autonomy. *Are we going to stifle that or make room for it?*

AT SOME POINT, I HAD TO PHYSICALLY LET GO OF MY DAUGHTER'S BIKE, OR SHE NEVER WOULD HAVE LEARNED TO RIDE IT ON HER OWN.

Preteens are at an age where developmentally (but not experientially) they are ready to start taking ownership of their faith, their relationships, their spirituality, and their lives. At some point, we must let go and let them take ownership of their Christianity.

The first essential of Intentional Preteen Ministry is a commitment to *letting go of the bike*. That means we create ministries where preteens are allowed—or, even better, ENCOURAGED—to use their new mental, physical, social, and emotional abilities to discover their own walk with God. It also means we expect some serious messing up as preteens stumble forward into ownership. We cheer them on for the two steps forward rather than scolding them when they fall. We're ready to dust a preteen off when he seriously messes up, smile at him reassuringly, and say, "You want to try this again? You've got it!"

ESSENTIAL 2: RUN BESIDE

Even though her birthday was still two months away, Savannah enlisted her younger brother's help to set things up in the backyard for her party. She was so excited. That's what you get when you let go of the bike: excited preteens. Preteens who take ownership and find ways to make things happen. Preteens like Savannah.

And preteens like Jeff.

JEFF WAS A SIXTH GRADER WITH A LOT OF ENERGY AND PERSONALITY.

He was a natural leader who wavered between wanting to stand in the shadows just outside of whatever activity was going on and wanting to lead the activities himself. Usually, he was more comfortable taking a spot in the background.

For just under three years, Jeff had been a part of StepUp, a leadership and discipleship program for preteens at our church. Around 15-25% of our regularly attending preteens participate in StepUp each year. In their third year of participation, preteens get to design and develop their very own ministry.

As Jeff was entering this final phase of the program, he asked to meet with me for yogurt. I asked Pastor Chris, who works with sixth graders, if he'd like to come along. We met up with Jeff for what I thought was going to be a time of hanging out. Instead, Jeff pulled out his cell phone and presented Chris and I with the tiniest slideshow I've ever seen. I'm not even sure how Jeff did it, but he put together a presentation on his phone about a ministry idea he'd been developing. The idea he presented on that small, cracked screen was to create a store within our preteen ministry space that would sell things like hats, t-shirts, and wristbands. The money earned would go to an orphanage in Mexico where our sixth graders serve each year.

Jeff had priced out how much it would cost to start the store and how much money he could make in the first year. He had the whole thing mapped out, and he did it all by himself. Over the two years he had already been in StepUp, Jeff had learned that we were probably going to listen to his idea and take him seriously. He knew he was in a ministry where we not only tolerate, but encourage, preteens to take risks and try "dangerous" things that will glorify God.

Jeff was excited. He was involved. He was using his brainpower and his time, devoting it toward developing something that could impact the Church and the world.

This is what I want: excited preteens. This is why we "let go."

HOWEVER...

Danger lurks when we create an environment like this for preteens.

When we let go of a literal bike—especially the first time—the mailboxes and potholes and cars parked on the side of the street magically become magnets for our new, wobbly riders.

There are dangers when we let go:

- Savannah's birthday idea could be a complete failure.
- Jeff's idea could cost our ministry serious money. He wanted to buy something like $2,000 worth of wristbands (because that was the best deal).

Remember, preteens are ready developmentally, but not experientially—and not emotionally, either. As the Association for Middle Level Education (AMLE) puts it, "emotional variability makes young adolescents at risk of making decisions with negative consequences." "While young adolescents start to consider complex moral and ethical questions, they tend to be unprepared to cope with them."[3]

Preteens are in a precarious place. On the one hand, we must let them spread their wings if they are going to grow up. On the other hand, they're likely to do some damage when they spread their wings for the first time. An excited preteen won't stay excited if she ends up in the hospital, or if his ideas end up as a massive, embarrassing failure. Remember, preteens are ready, but they're not ready.

When teaching somebody to ride a bike, we don't just let go. We also run beside.

AFTER THAT MEETING, PASTOR CHRIS RAN BESIDE JEFF.

- He helped Jeff come up with a more reasonable inventory.
- He helped Jeff sort the crummy merchandise websites from the quality ones.

---

3   Caskey, Micki and Anfara, Jr., Vincent A. "Developmental Characteristics of Young Adolescents." Association for Middle Level Education. Published October 2014. https://www.amle.org/BrowsebyTopic/WhatsNew/WNDet/TabId/270/ArtMID/888/ArticleID/455/Developmental-Characteristics-of-Young-Adolescents.aspx.

- He helped Jeff figure out where and how to set up the store so that it functioned well.

Chris didn't own the store, though. This was COMPLETELY Jeff's ministry. Just look at the picture on the door of the ~~closet~~ Elevate Store:

Our Founder
Elevate Store

Notice that it's not a picture of Chris. It's the picture of a preteen who is both shy and bold—who is both ready and not ready to open a store where Jesus' love shines bright as he raises money for an orphanage in Mexico.

We didn't just let go of the bike. Chris ran beside. He met with Jeff every Wednesday for 30 minutes or so to discuss what tweaks needed to be made to the store or what new products he wanted to start selling. Jeff even enlisted the help of other sixth graders to operate the store. He held a design contest amongst all the 4th-6th graders; you can see the resulting t-shirt in the picture above.

RUNNING BESIDE MEANS THAT I'M AN EVER-PRESENT GUIDE ON THE JOURNEY, BUT THAT IT NEVER BECOMES MY JOURNEY.

Running beside means that my wife and I offer to help Savannah think through her birthday plans. We don't make too many suggestions, as great as they may be. We allow this to be her process. Running beside means we ask questions that Savannah doesn't know to ask yet, because of her limited experience; but it doesn't mean we answer them for her. These can be questions like...

- Savannah, have you thought of asking your best friend, Brianna, to help you plan the party?
- Savannah, if you went to a party, what would you rather do: play your favorite game or play your least favorite game?
- Savannah, what if your friends decide they don't want to go along with your plan? What if they'd rather just hang out and talk, and they refuse to play? What would you do then?

Running beside means supporting where needed, perceiving when the bike is so wobbly that it's about to fall over and grabbing on to the handlebars, helping to make some correction, and then letting go again...until, finally, we can let go and watch as a kid confidently rides his or her OWN bike.

RUNNING BESIDE CAN BE EXHAUSTING AND TRICKY.

When teaching somebody to ride a literal bike, you might let go and grab on a dozen times before you finally let go and stop running. As a preteen starts to explore his or her own walk with God, there's no handbook telling leaders exactly when to grab on and when to allow for a little wobble room.

A sixth-grade boy who's been singing at the top of his lungs every week since kindergarten stops singing during worship time. Do you say anything? How much room do you give this preteen to not worship? What if he starts hanging out in the back of the room during worship or sits down? What if he starts distracting others? When exactly do you step in?

A fourth-grade girl is choosing friends who are causing her relationship with God to fade into the background. Do you talk to her parents about this? Do you risk her rejection by challenging her decisions? Do you stay silent and trust that God's plan is to resolve this without your involvement?

Letting Go is simple to understand: it's taking your hands off the situation and allowing the preteen to take ownership.

Running Beside is a little more complicated and involves some deeper thinking on the part of a ministry leader.

Run Beside involves these five things:

1. Be Present
2. Perceive
3. Pray
4. Coach
5. Catch and Release

Let's take these one at a time.

BE PRESENT

In a literal bike lesson, when an instructor lets go for the first time, the "being present" is easy to see. The teacher isn't standing at the end of the street; he's not half a block away texting friends while the brand-new bike rider is about to fall. No. The teacher is physically there, running in proximity to the student.

This aspect of preteen discipleship is why regular volunteers are key! I'm not interested in warm bodies who serve irregularly—I'm interested in leaders who walk with the preteens in our ministry. Of course, there's a balance when it comes to being present. There is a time when it becomes inappropriate and weird for me to run beside a bike rider who's shooting me dirty looks, as if to say, "I've got this." Being present can become creepy if we push ourselves on a preteen or family beyond what they perceive as being helpful.

It's important to develop relationships with parents and preteens, and to be on the lookout for signs that our presence is not welcomed (in which case it might be time to just Let Go & Not Run Beside, Or Let Go & Run a Few Paces Behind). At times, this is difficult to figure out. Exactly how much pursuing are we to do? Even when we know somebody needs help, our help may not be welcomed.

In preteen ministry, we take whatever opportunities we can find to do spiritual pursuit *if we think it will be helpful*. We stay present in the lives of our preteens. We hang out before service with them, doing activities that allow us to initiate conversations. We ask them questions about how they're doing in their relationships with God. We follow up when we haven't seen a preteen for a while, or when they've been going to big church with their parents. "How's Jonah doing?" We might ask a parent.

Being present is a necessary part of running beside.

PERCEIVE

Whereas being present puts us in proximity to a bike rider, perceiving keeps our eyes and mind on what's happening. Perceiving is about using our physical and spiritual senses to figure out WHY things are happening and HOW we need to respond.

In preteen ministry, perceiving is essential. When we see behaviors, we need to go beyond simply seeing what's on the surface—we need to ask ourselves "What's really going on for this preteen?"

If we aren't perceiving what's really going on, it's hard to know when or how to step in. If we aren't being intentionally perceptive, we can be blindsided when, one day, the preteen who "loved God so much" is no longer interested in being in church at all.

PRAY

Our inner conversations with God are critical as we interpret what we're perceiving. When we neglect to speak to God or listen to His Holy Spirit, our effectiveness takes a nosedive. "Apart from me you can do nothing," says Jesus in John 15:5 (NIV). In that same verse, Jesus tells us this: "If you remain in me and I in you, you will bear much fruit." When we abide in Jesus and go to Him with our requests, we're poised for God-honoring success in ministry.

This is why we ask God for the wisdom to understand what's happening for our preteens. We want to be able to see beyond behaviors to the underlying reasons so that we know how to respond. God knows all these things already, so why not just ask Him for help? Even if I'm present and perceiving, I'm not always certain or correct about what to do next. However, God's wisdom is infinite and available to me, and I do much better as a preteen leader when I rely on His ideas rather than my own.

Quick prayers in moments of ministry have helped me know what to say to a preteen. God's voice is the one I want these kids to hear, not mine. Extended times of prayer have helped me know whether I should call a parent or not call a parent.

In all situations, God's ideas are the best. In all situations, perceiving is valuable, but prayer is critical.

COACH

When somebody is learning to ride a physical bike and they get a little wobbly, we usually don't benefit them the most by grabbing the handlebars. Coaching somebody toward figuring out what to do is much more helpful than doing it for them. As the saying goes, "Give me a fish and I'll eat for a day. Teach me to fish and I'll eat for a lifetime."

We want to move progressively in our coaching:

FROM

Direct coaching: "Straighten up the handlebar. Lean to the left more."

TO

Indirect coaching: "What do you need to do? How can you fix this problem?"

Coaching preteens means helping them figure out what they need to do for themselves. As we are present, perceiving, praying, God will often help us know exactly what to do to show a preteen how to draw closer to Him. With coaching, we can help preteens discover strategies that will help them decipher what to do in the next situation—even if they're all alone. Intervention is immediate and efficient, but coaching is long-lasting and powerful.

CATCH & RELEASE

There are times when coaching isn't working and we simply need to step in. I think an example will be helpful here.

On Sunday, sixth-grade Kathy was leaning against the wall and messing around with a friend during our time of worship. From the front of the room, I made eye contact and *COACHED* her with an expression which begged her to answer the question, "What's the appropriate way to respond right now, Kathy?"

Kathy straightened up and focused on God for about half a minute. Then, out of the corner of my eye, I could perceive that she was back at it with her friend. I sensed that she was simply being lazy. She knows the importance of worship. She knows the expectation God has when it comes to worship. None of the other leaders in the room noticed what was going on, so, with a nod to the rest of the worship team, I left the stage as they continued leading and took Kathy and her friend into the hallway.

I told her that she wouldn't be allowed to be a distraction to her friends during worship, and that she needed to take some time by herself in the hallway to think through her actions. I explained that her friend and I were going to step back into the room, and she needed to stay there for a few moments to consider what appropriate behavior would be for somebody her age during worship time. It wasn't a time to coach. It wasn't a time to let Kathy spread her wings. I figuratively grabbed back onto the bike in that moment.

There are moments in which we need to grab the bike and say, "I'm the authority here, and I'm going to be in charge right now."

Here's the thing, though. We must RELEASE! We must catch AND RELEASE.

In those moments when we perceive that a reset is needed, it's okay. You're the boss, applesauce. Take charge. Remember, though, to let go again. 1 Peter 5:2-3 (NIV) says, "Be shepherds of God's flock that is under your care, watching over them—not because you must, but because you are willing, as God wants you to be...not lording it over those entrusted to you..."

I invited Kathy to come back into the room after our conversation, when she was ready to join the worship time. I didn't stand with her or have another leader stand with her. I RELEASED. I did watch her out of the corner of my eye, though.

JACOB WAS A FIFTH-GRADE BOY IN MY SMALL GROUP.

Putting all five steps together, here's an example of how I ran beside Jacob:

1. **Be Present:** As his Small Group leader, I was with Jacob just about every week. Our Small Group sat together during service and did things together outside of service, too, such as watching movies or going to each other's sporting events. In other words, I was present in Jacob's life.

2. **Perceive:** For a few weeks, it seemed that Jacob had stopped participating as much as he had been. I couldn't be sure, but he seemed disinterested in what was being taught. He stopped asking questions about the lessons and, during response time, I noticed he wasn't engaged like he used to be. His answers to questions during Small Group time were shallow. I perceived that maybe Jacob was struggling to go any deeper in his relationship with God.

3. **Pray:** Sitting next to him one Wednesday night in service, I inquired of God what I should do about the things I was noticing. I had the distinct impression that I should say something to Jacob right then.

4. **Coach:** "Jacob," I leaned over and said, "How would you say your relationship with God is lately?" Jacob looked back at me and responded by scrunching up his mouth, raising his left hand and tilting it side to side. I speak fluent preteen, so I knew this meant, "My relationship with God is lukewarm right now." I nodded and said, "Jacob, do you want to stay where you are, or do you want to be excited about your relationship with God?" He replied, "I want to be excited." "Okay," I said. "Here's what I do when I'm feeling this way. I force myself to participate even when I don't feel like it. I read my Bible more. I listen to Christian music more. Jacob, I know God wants to be closer with you, too. Maybe you need to make more of an effort."

5. **Catch & Release:** In this case, I didn't need to intercede any further. This quick conversation seemed to have an effect—within a week, I could see that Jacob was back on track, even when he didn't think I was watching.

ELI RAN BESIDE.

One thing Patrick Snow likes to point out in the story of Samuel's calling is what Eli did the morning after he "let go of the bike" and released Samuel to commune with God on his own.

"In the morning, Eli called him and said, 'Samuel, my son.'
Samuel answered, 'Here I am.'
'What was it he said to you?' Eli asked." (1 Samuel 3:16-17)

Eli didn't just let go of the bike. He ran beside. He followed up the next day and asked Samuel what happened.

This is what Intentional Preteen Ministry looks like.

It's an equation:

Let Go + Run Beside = Intentional Preteen Ministry

If you're more accustomed to Children's Ministry, you may have difficulty with the letting go part of the equation. If you're more accustomed to Youth Ministry, the running beside part might be more of a challenge. Intentional Preteen Ministry is a blend of the two. Preteens are ready developmentally, but not experientially, to take their first steps toward faith ownership. Because of this, we do both.

We let go. And we run beside.

ESSENTIAL 3:
INVITE PRETEENS TO TAKE RISKS IN A SAFE ENVIRONMENT

The mental image of somebody letting go of a bike and running beside can be helpful when thinking of how to lead an Intentional Preteen Ministry; it's a picture in which the leader strikes a meaningful balance between safety and challenge.

Having an Intentional Preteen Ministry means monitoring and evaluating to ensure that challenge and safety are present simultaneously in good measure. Sometimes, it feels a little like having two dials.

Both knobs are important. If either is turned too low or high, we aren't creating an optimal discipleship experience for preteens.

The Importance of Challenge

In an environment that is safe but not challenging, preteens become restless. They need a purpose and a level of challenge that keeps them engaged if they're going to grow. If we aren't creating a program and an environment in which we're challenging preteens, they'll often challenge us. Often, a misbehaving preteen is a bored (but "safe") preteen.

The Importance of Safety

In an environment that is highly challenging without a good measure of safety, some preteens can become withdrawn or fearful. They may not take on challenges in which they would have found success if they'd taken a risk.

The lower the safety level, the less preteens are *willing* to take REAL risks.

The higher the safety level, the less preteens are *actually* taking REAL risks.

We are concerned about the physical safety of our preteens, but we need to keep an eye on emotional safety, as well. For many preteens—especially the older ones—being embarrassed in front of peers can be a far greater source of pain than breaking a bone.

An Intentional Preteen Ministry is one in which kids feel safe as we challenge them to spread their wings and try new things.

Creating a safe and challenging environment requires balance. Long-term growth won't happen without risk. In an environment where risk is encouraged, growth is the result.

THE PRETEEN YEARS ARE A TIME WHEN KIDS ARE EXCITED TO TRY NEW AND CHALLENGING THINGS.

It's critical, therefore, that we focus on what happens when preteens try something that doesn't work out so well. If they feel unsupported or rejected when they don't succeed, their excitement to try new things will quickly disappear, and their growth will slow. An Intentional Preteen Ministry is one in which failure doesn't equal condemnation.

A few days ago, my preteen son grabbed an unused roll of painters' tape I had purchased. He used the entire roll to create cool-looking blue shoes for himself. He was being creative, but he didn't ask permission to use the tape. He took a risk and tried out his burgeoning ability to explore possibilities; in the process, he made a mistake. Ten-year-old kids are good at making mistakes.

Our response as parents was important, because it had the potential to make him feel condemned to the point that he might never again look for resources to use creatively (after all, creative utilization is something he can hone to glorify God). If he doesn't feel safe to make mistakes, he may not take as many risks. Just as we do in ministry, we want to create a home environment in which our kids are both challenged to grow and safe to make mistakes.

Honestly, I'm not sure if our response to the used tape was one that struck a good balance of providing him with correction and emotional safety; but I pray that it was.

Funny—but true—side note: my son is sitting across the desk from me as I'm typing this, finger-painting with watercolors (his idea). I watched him do something that made me smile right after I wrote the last paragraph: one of the colors in his paint tray was too wet and he needed something to dry it out a bit. He noticed an envelope sitting near my computer and grabbed it as a creative way to soak up the paint. I didn't make eye contact with him, but noticed him pause just after he grabbed the mail piece. He stopped in his tracks and asked, "Dad, do you need this for anything?"

Thank you, God, for answering my prayer.

Our response to his blue-shoe mistake challenged him toward growth, instead of leading to the end of his creative experimentation with resources.

If we're going to encourage preteens to keep their adventurous, exploring ways—which can ultimately help them take steps into God-glorifying faith ownership—then it's essential that we create an environment in which failure isn't condemned.

I'm reminded of a Bible principle in Proverbs 28:3 (NIV): "A ruler who oppresses the poor is like a driving rain that leaves no crops." Rain is good for helping crops to grow, but a driving rain will kill the crops. This is the way challenge and safety work in helping to create an environment where preteens thrive; a good amount of both is necessary for growth, but too much of either, and nothing grows.

It's all about adjusting the safety and challenge dials as we search for that optimal balance.

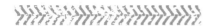

THERE ARE SEVERAL FACTORS TO CONSIDER WHEN THINKING ABOUT HOW MUCH CHALLENGE AND HOW MUCH SAFETY TO PROVIDE TO PRETEENS.

Age/Maturity

As time goes on and preteens move from 4th to 5th to 6th grade, we want to gradually turn up the challenge dial and turn down the safety dial, so that we're creating an environment for optimal growth. This will prepare them to step into their next phase of ministry and development.

By contemplating the challenges of the teenage years and the lack of safety measures most teenagers have in place, we can make the preteen years a time in which we gradually prepare them for what's to come.

Engagement

A low engagement level from preteens typically means it's time to adjust one or both knobs.

Usually, a bored group of preteens is an unchallenged group of preteens. When I start to notice glazed eyes, yawns, bored frowns during service, I see it as an indication that it's time to turn up the challenge dial.

I might:

- challenge the preteens to a new service project
- create an activating Bible reading challenge fin which Small Groups can compete
- increase the leadership opportunities for preteens within service
- open the microphone so that preteens can step forward and share what God's doing in their lives
- say something more direct, like, "You look bored. This isn't what Church should look like. We're all going to take a moment right now to be silent and think of a challenge that Jesus might want to give to our group today. I'm going to call on a few of you to share."

There are countless ways to challenge the preteens in your group. When you see unengaged, bored kids, it's usually a sign that it's time to turn up the challenge knob.

However, low engagement can also mean that the safety knob needs to be turned up. This is a different type of disengagement than the bored, sleepy type. This type looks more like holding back for fear of failure. If you have preteens not raising their hands to participate, or hesitating to play games, perhaps they're concerned that they'll be ridiculed if they make a mistake. If you had low numbers at your last preteen event, one possibility is that the preteens didn't feel safe coming. Pay attention for this type of disengagement.

Turning up the safety knob involves perceiving your preteens' concerns and then finding ways to address them. This will typically lead to increased engagement...but be careful. We aren't training preteens to be engaged with kingdom-building activity only within our ministries. We are training them for success *in an unsafe world*. When it becomes clear that preteens feel safe engaging within your ministry, it's time to turn up the challenge knob and commission them to do something for God outside the safety of your ministry.

Capacity

Another factor to consider is the mental and emotional capacities of the preteens we are leading. Paula Mazza is a friend of mine, and the founder of *PreteenMentalHealth.com*. When it comes to striking a balance of challenge and risk for preteens with mental health concerns, here's her perspective:

> *With preteens there is an internal dialogue that may or may not match the external evidence. This dialogue might not be fact-based, however, it is experienced as very real. While this is true of most preteens to some degree, it tends to be amplified in preteens with underlying mental health concerns.*
>
> *For example, imagine asking a preteen a question and while you are actively and enthusiastically listening to their answer, you inadvertently yawn once or twice simply because you haven't been sleeping well. It's possible that the preteen is so busy sharing their thoughts that they don't even notice. However, a preteen who is struggling with depression will not only notice that yawn but internalize it in a way*

that feeds their depression with thoughts like "I knew it. Even my church leader is bored with me," or "See? I am so unimportant that even the adults can barely stay awake."

Although the yawn was benign, it was received differently.

It's also important to note that this atypical thinking is more common than you might realize. The National Alliance of Mental Health reports that in the United States, 1 in 6 youth aged 6-17 years old experience a mental health disorder. They also report that 50% of all lifetime mental illnesses begin showing symptoms in people before the age of fourteen years. (www.nami.org/mhstats)

In creating a space that is both physically safe and socially/emotionally safe, it is important to recognize that while something might appear safe to the common eye, it may not feel safe to a depressive preteen. Likewise, something that feels like a mild risk to most may be experienced as a paralyzing risk for a preteen struggling with anxiety. Awareness and training will help the church leader recognize the signs of mental illness and adjust their approach to ministry in a way that is inclusive of all states of brain health.

IT'S DIFFICULT (PERHAPS IMPOSSIBLE) TO GET THE BALANCE RIGHT ALL THE TIME.

In those seasons when we do, preteens are challenged to reach toward their potential with confidence.

Here are three methods we've discovered along the way that create safety for our preteens and simultaneously challenge them to grow.

Method 1: Small Bites

Each year, the preteens on our leadership team take a trip to the Tenderloin of San Francisco. While there, our 4th-6th graders make sandwiches and deliver them to homeless people on the streets. They help run a Saturday morning church service for kids in the area. They organize clothes at a thrift store that ministers to drug addicts. It's an incredibly challenging and eye-opening experience for them. The challenge knob is turned way up for this one.

However, we surround the event with a thick layer of safety. We typically have about a 2:3 ratio of leaders to preteens. We shorten the duration of the trip, driving to San Francisco early in the morning and returning the afternoon of the same day. We partner with an established ministry in the Tenderloin that's located just across the street from the police station, and the organization provides additional staff, guidance, and safety. We spend about forty minutes each Sunday, for four weeks leading up to the trip, preparing the preteens for what they're likely to see, hear, and smell, and teaching them how they can process what they're going to experience.

After our day in the Tenderloin, we sit in a large circle and talk about what they experienced. The following Sunday, we spend another forty minutes processing it even more. Our strategy for this mission trip has been to take a challenging experience for preteens and break it up into small pieces that they can digest. We don't just throw them into the deep end of the mission trip pool and see if they sink or swim. We start by inviting them to put one toe in the water, and then slowly move through the shallow end.

Here's another example of the "small bites" strategy: about twice a year, we have a preteen band lead worship during a service. However, we take three or four weeks to practice and prepare them for a single song. Sometimes, an adult drummer will stand by the drums to help during the service should the wheels start to come off. We have adult leaders in the crowd being "led" by the preteens on the stage, but these leaders are ready to jump in and sing loudly should the preteen singer onstage forget where the song is supposed to go next.

We've been able to develop preteen musicians and worship leaders by taking a complex, challenging activity and breaking it down into bite-size components.

Method 2: Create a Culture of Emotional Safety

"For the Spirit God gave us does not make us timid, but gives us power, love and self-discipline." —2 Timothy 1:7 (NIV)

When the Holy Spirit permeates your leadership team and your ministry, safety and challenge are optimized. Let's first invite the Holy Spirit to be in us and to be present in everything that happens in our ministry space. Then, as preteens have success and develop confidence, we can challenge them to do God-glorifying things in a less safe environment, such as their neighborhoods or schools. They'll come to realize that the same Holy Spirit who marks their time in your ministry can mark their lives wherever they go.

Within your ministry space, there are few practical things you may feel led to do as preteens are growing in their confidence in Christ. Perhaps you can challenge a preteen to put together and deliver a 2-minute sermon for the whole group, *but* you allow a friend or leader to stand with her while she does it. Perhaps you can challenge a preteen to stand out in front of the church and welcome visitors, *but* you allow a friend or leader to stand shoulder-to-shoulder with him as he takes on this "scary" task. It's easier for preteens to take on big challenges if they are surrounded and supported by people they trust.

We also help to create a culture of emotional safety for preteens by taking risks ourselves. If we are willing to try new things—things at which we may fail—we send the message that our ministry is a safe place to take risks. You and your volunteers can play a big part in turning up the safety knob by doing silly, potentially embarrassing, risky things.

This is especially effective if you have teenagers serving in your ministry who understand this dynamic. We had a teenage leader dress up as "The Magnificent Macaroni" and perform death-defying stunts like jumping over a feather on his broomstick. As people laughed and cheered for Brett's success, we were creating a culture of emotional safety in our group (and a great set-up for our lesson that day, too). You might try something new, like playing an instrument, leading worship, or learning a new magic trick that may not work out. Let them see that success isn't a guarantee for you, and that this reality doesn't stop you from trying new things that may help you to glorify God. As preteens see that leaders—especially younger leaders—are willing to take risks, they come to understand that your ministry space is a safe one.

There's another task involved in creating a culture of emotional safety for your preteens: as a shepherd, you carry both a staff and a rod. The staff helps you draw the sheep along in the right direction. The rod helps you keep the wolves away. Creating a culture of emotional safety will sometimes require disciplining those "wolves" who are discouraging risk-taking. When a scoffer laughs at a risk-taker who messes up, I immediately put a stop to it. I take a strong stance and make it clear that risk-taking will NOT get negative attention—teasing somebody, however, will.

Creating a culture of emotional safety takes patience, vulnerability, and a determination to protect the flock. It also takes a team of leaders and volunteers who are willing and equipped to do the same. Learning together with your leaders about how to create emotional safety for preteens is a huge step in the right direction.

Additionally, creating Small Groups that are actually SMALL (we prefer four, five, or six in a group), and in which preteens are known and supported by caring leaders, has been an essential element of our strategy. It's in these Small Groups that preteens have the greatest sense of safety in risk-taking. In groups where they feel emotionally protected, they take big risks as they share challenges, confess shortcomings, ask important questions, and allow themselves to be vulnerable.

As your ministry becomes a place of greater emotional safety, you'll be facilitating preteens' willingness to take meaningful risks in their walk with Christ.

Method 3: Simulate Real-Life Challenges

A simulation takes a real-life experience and removes some of the risk. Before flying an actual fighter jet in battle, a simulation allows a pilot to experience what it will be like without the real-life consequences.

There are several ways to simulate real-life challenges for the preteens you lead.

- If you're teaching a lesson about defending their faith, you can have pairs of preteens come up with skits showing a real-life situation in which somebody's faith is being challenged.
- If you're teaching about how to pray for people's needs, you can have preteens take turns praying aloud for needs that you write on strips of paper and pull out of a hat.
- If you want to teach preteens to live out the principles Jesus taught in the Parable of the Talents, you can give three preteens a ten-dollar bill each. You can ask them to report back the next week and explain what they did with the money you gave them.

When you want to invite preteens to do something challenging, try simulating the experience first.

IT'S VITAL THAT WE ARE CHALLENGING OUR PRETEENS TO DO GREAT THINGS FOR THE KINGDOM.

Nothing insults many preteens more than when adults underestimate what they can accomplish.

Preteens can:

- write worship songs,
- lead Small Groups,
- run the tech booth,
- lead worship,
- make phone calls to kids who are missing,
- stand in front of the church and greet visitors,
- lead others to Christ,
- find good, Biblical answers to difficult, complex moral issues, and
- so much more!

Challenge your preteens to greater things, and they will respond. If the experience is a safe one, they will grow in their confidence and boldness to live for Christ.

Pause a moment before leaving this chapter and think about your ministry to preteens. Think about the two dials again:

Consider these questions:

- How are you doing in these two areas?
- What adjustments need to be made in your ministry?
- How do you know?

ESSENTIAL 4:
GIVE CHOICES AND SHARE POWER

When we share power with the preteens in our ministries by giving them choices, we're completely changing the dynamic of their relationship with the Church. We're changing their understanding of who they are in the Church, and who they are in Christ.

As we start to allow preteens to have power and choice within our ministries—in little ways and in big ways—we're saying, "Hey. You have a brain that's developing, and we want to help you learn how to handle these amazing, emerging capabilities that God is giving you." Preteens have a developing desire to exert power and to make meaningful, consequential choices. If they aren't trained in how to do these things in early adolescence, when they're more open to correction and instruction, it can prove disastrous later, when they're teenagers.

Imagine this: one day, you're given a license to drive, but you've had no instruction. You've never had a learner's permit. You go straight from sitting in the back seat to sitting in the driver's seat, without any restrictions or any help. Imagine this happening at a time in your life when you think that you're invincible and that adults aren't all that smart. When preteens go without opportunities to make choices and have power when in their faith walk, they're less likely to experience success when they get older.

In an Intentional Preteen Ministry, you have the opportunity to sit in the copilot seat for a few years—to help young adolescents discover how to make their own choices and exert their own power while they're still willing to receive guidance.

I TOLD YOU ABOUT SAVANNAH'S PLANS FOR HER TWELFTH BIRTHDAY PARTY.

What I didn't tell you is this: besides being her pastor, I'm also her dad.

After much discussion between my wife and me about the risks and rewards of her plan, we decided to release control of the party to her. She wanted to have a birthday party with what we considered to be a bizarre schedule of playing everybody's least favorite games, but we decided to stand back and let her make that choice.

The result was positive.

Her friends came over and had a great time playing the games they normally hate. It worked for her friend group, because they know her and are easygoing preteens who are open to new and unusual experiences. Allowing Savannah to have power and control in that situation was affirming for her, and has helped her to walk with confidence in her ability to accomplish great things.

It's taken me a while to write this book. Savannah is thirteen years old as this book goes to print. Now, she serves in our preteen ministry as a leader, and she's great at creating and leading activities. I'm glad we let go of the bike and allowed her to have some power and control when she was eleven.

WHEN WE GIVE PRETEENS POWER AND CHOICES, EVEN IN THE LITTLE THINGS IN MINISTRY, IT CAN BE A BIG DEAL FOR THEM.

They light up with enthusiasm, because you're meeting them where they are developmentally. Preteens are wired to explore possibilities. We can help them learn to do this wisely, but we must let them do it. We must let go of the bike.

Maybe you've had this experience: a preteen will make a choice—one she knows is the wrong choice—and stick to it, because it's HERS. If you've ever seen the movie Spider-Man: Into the Spider-Verse, the main character is in seventh or eighth grade. He has an untied shoe for most of the movie; when people question him about it, he responds, "It's a choice."

This totally resonated with me. For the preteens I work with, it's often not important that the choice they're making is the RIGHT choice; the important thing for them is that it's THEIR choice. If I'm teaching a lesson to younger kids, I tell them, "This is what the Bible says. This is the example of Moses. This is what will please God." End of lesson. Bam. That's great.

When I start talking with preteens, however, I need to acknowledge that they may look at the choice that Moses (or whoever) made, or what God says, and then think, "Okay, that's one choice; but I'm going to choose something else. Because I can. Because I'm exploring possibilities."

We can acknowledge the reality of where preteens are developmentally in the way we talk to and teach them. We can help them begin to think about their choices as something they own. We can start to provide training in making choices that they will feel good about later.

WHEN KIDS ARE YOUNGER, THEY TEND TO BE MORE CONCERNED WITH MAKING CHOICES THAT WILL PLEASE THE ADULTS IN THEIR LIVES.

As they approach their teenage years, however, it's important to help preteens contemplate the kind of choices that THEY are pleased with making themselves. I want to help preteens discover the joy of making choices that honor God. This joy is only theirs when the decision to honor God is a decision that they are making of their own volition.

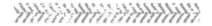

HERE ARE SIX POWER/CHOICE EXPERIMENTS WE'VE TRIED WITH THE PRETEENS IN OUR MINISTRY.

As you read each one, pause and consider how you can give power and choice to the preteens in your ministry, as well.

1. Check-in and Preservice

Even before service starts, we give preteens choice and power. At our check-in booth, we have preprinted name tags, and we encourage preteens to add to them by answering a question written on a small chalkboard. They write the answer to the "Question of the Day" directly on their name tag. The question can be, "What's your favorite month of the year?" or, "What's your favorite flavor of ice cream?" We even provide multiple colors of markers for them to choose from.

After they check in, we'll have several activities set up for them, as well. There's a "café," where they can grab a snack and talk with friends. There's usually a more active game, like dodgeball, and a quieter game like Uno. There's usually a craft project, too.

We provide preteens with choices from the very beginning of their experience each week. Even before service starts, we've communicated something powerful to them about who they are as a unique part of the Church—the body of Christ—and about their ability to be trusted with choice and power.

2. Un-Pirate Ships

Let's say you want to engage your preteens in a mission project. You could say, "We're going to raise money for such-and-such ministry."

That's one way to do it, but we've found it far more powerful to give preteens choices about who they're going to raise money for and to whom they're going to donate their time. We created something called Un-Pirate ships, where the preteens become the crew of an un-pirate ship. After presenting several options, they decide for themselves as a group where their un-pirate ship is going.

A regular pirate ship goes to a place with wealth and steals it, but an un-pirate ship takes wealth to a place that needs it. In their un-pirate crews, the preteens decide how much they're going to raise, how they're going to raise it, and where the money is going to be given. Then they set about doing it.

3. Naming

When I started the Intentional Preteen Ministry at Destiny Church, I let the preteens come up with the name of the ministry instead of creating it myself. This was the process:

- The first week, everybody could make suggestions by writing their ideas for ministry names on index cards.
- I took all of their suggestions and narrowed it down to three that the leaders and I could live with.

- The next week, the preteens voted on the name of THEIR ministry.

Our ministry is called Elevate! I probably could have come up with this name myself, but it's better because the preteens came up with it. From the beginning, preteens saw that they had ownership in this ministry.

Each year, we do something similar for our Small Groups. We let the preteens choose their Small Groups. As long as they're behaving with the people they've chosen, they can stay in those groups.

They also get to name their Small Groups. Of course, we have interesting group names, like the following (these are all real):

- Savage Toenails
- Spicy Doggos
- Cozy Grandpa Jerald

Tell me what would be more meaningful to a fifth grader: being able to invite friends at school to come join the 4th Grade Green Team in Destiny Preteens, or being able to invite friends at school to join the Savage Toenails in Elevate?

If you said the first option, you're thinking like an adult. When ministering to preteens, we must start releasing ministry control, or else it becomes clear to them that this whole Church thing is ours, not theirs.

4. This or That

When our leadership team tried to figure out a way to make our announcements more engaging, the concept of "This or That" was born. Instead of announcing an upcoming event, we now give the preteens a choice. Here's an example of what this might sound like:

"It's time for 'This or That.' Coming up Friday, we have a game night at the church, but we aren't sure what kind of food to serve. Walk over to THIS wall if you want to have pizza. Walk over to THAT wall if you want BBQ hot dogs."

When we do "This or That," the preteens take ownership in the things we're announcing, and they're more likely to be engaged—to think of it as *their* event, instead of just one that the church is putting on *for* them.

Many times, in ministry, you may ask, "What should we do about this particular problem?" or, "How can we decorate this?" or, "What's the best use of this resource?" When we have questions like this, we often put it into the preteens' hands. This communicates to them our belief that they can start to make sound decisions, and that they are as much a part of the Church as we are.

5. Response Stations

At the end of a lesson, you may have a responsive activity planned. Maybe it's a worship song, a craft, or a written response to the message. If you're providing just one way of responding, a preteen who is exploring possibilities and wanting to exert power and control may think, "Yeah, I could do that. Or not. I could just talk with my friends instead."

Here's another approach: if you want to give a preteen three or four choices for how to respond at the end of a lesson, you might say, "You can do this over here, or you can do this over here, or you can do this over here." In choosing this approach, you're allowing each preteen to have power in deciding how he or she will respond to the message.

There are preteens who will not participate in Activity A when it's the only activity; but when there's Activities A, B, and C to choose from, that same preteen might choose Activity A, simply because it's now his choice.

It's significant for preteens to have power and choice in how they respond to messages. Through Response Stations, we see them start to take ownership of their responses to God's Word and His call on their lives.

6. Leadership

Even before our preteen ministry was separated from the children's ministry, one way in which we gave preteens choice and power was through a leadership program. They ran the tech booth, performed check in, helped lead worship, made announcements, and prayed at the end of the services. We've added other assignments throughout the years. Now, they stand in front of the church and greet people, looking for fourth, fifth and sixth graders to invite to our ministry. They set up before service. They clean up after service. They go on the one-day mission trip to the Tenderloin. They plan a volunteer appreciation Sunday. There are numerous ways preteens in our leadership program can serve the Church.

We're careful to ensure that parents don't sign them up for the leadership program. Likewise, we never have a leadership program where ALL kids are expected to participate. It's their choice whether they want to join.

Our leadership program continues to develop. It now consists of three phases:

- The first phase is **discipleship**.
- The second phase is learning and practicing **service skills and mentalities**, such as humbly cleaning after everybody leaves, or lovingly welcoming visitors and taking them on tours.
- In the third phase, the preteens **create their own ministry**. They propose an idea to the leaders, and we work with them to develop their own ministry within the Church. We've had preteens whose ministry is to do more obvious things, like serve in the preschool. Then, we've had out-of-the-box ideas. I told you about Jeff's store in Chapter 2, but there have been other creative ideas along the way, including starting an Elevate newsletter, creating a library of Christian books with a check-out system, and starting a drama group to create skits for lessons.

AMAZING THINGS HAPPEN WHEN WE GIVE THE PRETEENS IN OUR MINISTRY POWER AND CHOICES.

If we say, "This is how you're going to respond," and don't give preteens any choices, they are still going to explore their possibilities. They may be looking for ways to get out of doing the one thing you're telling them to do. That's just how they're wired.

But when we create a space in which we're helping preteens embrace choice and power as a way of glorifying God—a space in which we're trusting and empowering them with important decisions, and in which we're helping them learn from the consequences of those choices—they'll use their burgeoning capabilities to honor God in powerful and unique ways.

Just think about the potential that's locked within the preteens in your ministry!

What's a practical way in which you can provide your preteens with choice and power this month? It could be something as little as letting them decide what color flyer you're going to use to print a parent announcement, or it could be a much bigger project. Pause for a moment and jot down your thoughts on a piece of paper or in your phone's notes app.

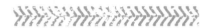

HOW CAN CHOICE AND POWER BE SHARED DURING SMALL GROUP TIME?

If you think about a traditional children's ministry approach to Small Group time, the leader brings the agenda to the group. Typically, this is a page of questions or instructions that the leader reads through, and the kids are supposed to respond.

With preteens, we've found that this kind of set up is when they mentally check out of the program. What really ministers to preteens is having choice and power within their Small Group discussion. One strategy we've used is asking questions at the end of a lesson and giving the preteens time to think about them in silence before going to Small Group. We might ask:

- What did God reveal to you during service?
- What questions do you have about today's lesson?

After preteens have thought through these questions, they're ready to bring the agenda and content to the Small Groups for themselves. This has proven to be extremely effective. When preteens own the conversation, they're much more likely to engage and internalize the content.

As we were developing the Deeply Rooted Curriculum for preteens, we wanted to find an engaging way to help preteens think about facing pressures in their lives, so they could have meaningful discussions about it in their Small Groups. We called the series "Diamonds" because if you have pressure and you have rock, you have the ingredients for a diamond. Preteens have pressure in their lives. If they have God's Word in their lives, then they have a rock, too. Together, these two things can make valuable "diamonds."

Knowing that preteens like to play games, we came up with the Diamond Collectors game for Small Group time. It's similar to the game Apples to Apples. In the Diamond Collectors deck, there are cards with pressures written on them. They say things like, "Do your homework" or, "Don't talk about Jesus." A preteen flips over a Pressure Card and reads it. He or she might say, "Okay, here's the pressure: 'Do your homework.'" Naturally, the other preteens will say things like, "Oh yeah. I face that pressure every day."

The preteens get the conversation going, not the leader. A group leader can facilitate the discussion by asking a question: "When have any of you faced this kind of pressure?" Next, the preteens look at the four Rock Cards they drew from the deck. Each Rock Card has a different Bible verse on it. They search their Rock Cards for one they think would help with this pressure. For instance, one of the preteens might lay down the Rock Card with Colossians 3:32 written on it: "Whatever you do, work heartily, as for the Lord and not for men."

After each player has chosen a Rock Card, they hand them to the preteen who read the pressure. That preteen reads all of the verses out loud and picks one that he or she thinks would be most helpful in turning the pressure into a diamond. Again, the Small Group leaders aren't controlling the conversation; they're merely facilitating the discussion. The preteens have power and choice as they discuss pressures in their lives and look for solutions from God's Word.

Think about this approach and how different this is to saying, "Here's a Bible verse, kids. How can you apply it when you have a lot of homework to do?" Intentional Preteen Ministry is different because Small Group time is structured so that the content is coming from the preteens.

IT CAN BE SCARY TO PUT POWER AND CHOICES INTO PRETEENS' HANDS, BECAUSE YOU DON'T KNOW WHAT YOU'RE GOING TO GET WHEN YOU DO.

Often, though, it turns out to be more amazing than what you could have imagined yourself. When we give preteens choices, their engagement level is exciting to be around. When you let go of a bike, the bike rider MIGHT wobble and fall over. They MIGHT head straight for a mailbox. But we don't let what MIGHT happen keep us from letting go.

Instead, we focus on the potential.

The potential is amazing for preteens when we let go and allow them to make choices and have power within our ministries. When this happens, the excitement that preteens have about Church, about God, and about taking ownership of their faith walk makes it worth the risk.

Do something a little frightening this week as you're developing your Intentional Preteen Ministry. Put some power and choices into the hands of your preteens, and see what happens as they take ownership!

ESSENTIAL 5:
IMPLEMENT ACTIVE LEARNING STRATEGIES

There's a big difference between engaging and entertaining.

If we're entertaining preteens, we're providing them with amusement or enjoyment. If we're engaging preteens, on the other hand, we're providing them with an opportunity to DO something. Entertainment is often passive. Engagement is always active.

Ministry is not, at its core, about entertainment. Ever. We're not in competition with Disney or our preteens' favorite YouTube videos. Entertainment can have value in the life of a preteen, but it is not one of the goals of Intentional Preteen Ministry. Engagement is.

There can be an argument made for having elements of entertainment in your ministry to preteens, for sure. Make them laugh. Have fun watching video clips together. Go ahead and entertain them in small or in big ways. Done well, there can be value in entertaining the Church. Remember, though, that, in a life of Christian faith and God-honoring works, being entertained does not have the same impact as being engaged.

HERE'S AN EXAMPLE THAT ILLUSTRATES THE DIFFERENCE BETWEEN ENGAGING AND ENTERTAINING.

A group of preteens from our ministry put on a play. They worked on it for months under the leadership of Pastor Chris Santos. Then, they performed it for the rest of our preteen ministry. It was a great performance that had a clear Gospel message. Afterward, I realized something. The actors were impacted by the experience in a much more profound way than the audience was. What was the difference? The audience was primarily entertained by the play. The actors were engaged in it.

Intentional Preteen Ministry creates experiences for preteens that are more like being in a play than watching a play—more like building the boat than sailing in it. It's more lab than lecture.

God is probably the focus of your ministry. Obviously, the spotlight should be shining on Him. The question is this: *who's holding the spotlight?* If the strategies you're using to teach are primarily video- or teacher-driven, it may be time to evaluate. Intentional Preteen Ministry is Christ-centric with ample invitations for preteens to "hold the spotlight" themselves as they engage and participate in the God-glorifying activity of the Church.

Intentional Preteen Ministry is about active engagement, not passive entertainment.

PRETEENS TEND TO BE ACTIVE LEARNERS.

The AMLE article, *Developmental Characteristics of Early Adolescents*, states this: "Early adolescents favor active over passive learning experiences and prefer interactions with peers during educational activities."[4]

The 1991 book, *Active Learning: Creating Excitement in the Classroom* by Bonwell and Eison coined the phrase "active learning." Here's how they define it: *"instructional activities involving students in doing things and thinking about what they're doing."*[5]

Active learning means that preteens are researching, writing, and delivering a sermon instead of simply hearing it. Then, afterward, they're thinking about what the experience taught them. Active learning involves creation, experimentation, and risk-taking. When preteens participate in active learning, they thrive! It meets them right where they are developmentally and helps them take steps into faith ownership.

Imagine preteens experiencing the Word of God as "alive and active" (Hebrews 4:12). Imagine preteens who are "doers of the word, and not hearers only" (James 1:22). It's like learning to ride a bike.

Learning to ride a bike is an active process. You don't learn by watching videos of people riding bikes or by hearing about people who rode bikes in the past. You must sit on the bike yourself to learn how to ride it. Finding your balance, learning to steer, and the whole-body coordination required isn't something you learn by observation. You learn it by doing.

---

4   Caskey, Micki and Anfara, Jr., Vincent A. "Developmental Characteristics of Young Adolescents." Association for Middle Level Education. Published October 2014. https://www.amle.org/BrowsebyTopic/WhatsNew/WNDet/TabId/270/ArtMID/888/ArticleID/455/Developmental-Characteristics-of-Young-Adolescents.aspx.

5   Bonwell, Charles C. and Eison, James A. *Active Learning: Creating Excitement in the Classroom.* Jossey-Bass, January 31, 1991.

Faith ownership and walking with Jesus is the same. It isn't something we master by passively observing. True faith ownership requires active learning. Think about 1 Samuel 3, in which Eli coaches Samuel into owning his relationship with God. Eli doesn't launch into a lecture about having a relationship with God. Instead, he facilitates an active learning environment for Samuel, so that he can experience God for Himself.

ACTIVE LEARNING DOESN'T NECESSARILY REQUIRE A LOT OF PHYSICAL MOVEMENT; BUT WHEN IT DOES, PHYSICAL MOVEMENT IS LIKE GASOLINE ON THE FIRE OF ACTIVE LEARNING.

Inside the heads of early adolescents, chemicals that the brain produces can build up. If you've ever seen a distracted, fidgety preteen, you may be seeing chemical build-up in his or her brain. Physical movement gives preteens a way to release some of the energy that this chemical build-up creates, allowing preteens to engage in a more focused time of learning after they move.

Here's a truth I've seen play out in our ministry time and time again: including moments of physical involvement increases preteens' ability to stay focused for prolonged periods. If you get preteens to stand up, run around the building, and then sit back down, they are better able to focus on the lesson being taught for a longer period of time.

I've seen this to be especially true in our Wednesday night programming. Preteens have a different energy on a midweek evening than they do on a Sunday morning. Many of them have spent most of their Wednesday sitting still in a controlled classroom environment, and the chemicals are building up like crazy in their brains. When we take that into account, and plan the first half hour of the evening to be high-energy and full of physical activity, our preteens are way more settled and focused when the second and more serious half of service begins.

Some people think that planning physical activity will just get preteens riled up—that it will only result in a struggle to get them to calm down; but this struggle can be mitigated by having clear expectations and enforcing them. We've done water games, massive obstacle courses, 30 minutes of slime-based activities, and large active games at the beginning of services. You might think these things would cause our preteens to be unfocused for the rest of the night, but my experience has been the opposite. They "get their energy out," and then, as a result, they're able to engage with a lesson that requires a bit more focused attention.

Patrick Snow, director at Christ In Youth, has pointed out that something as simple as having everybody scream in the middle of a lesson, or having preteens stand up and move around the room briefly, can help to give them a "chemical release break."

These moments of energy release don't need to be random, though. They can tie into a lesson. Here are some examples:

- When we ask questions in a lesson, sometimes we'll have preteens go to different corners of the room: "If you think the answer is A, go over here; B, go over here; C, go over here; D, go over here."
- We'll create a continuum across the room. For instance, when we teach the lesson in the Diamond series about pressure from authorities, we'll say, "This wall over here symbolizes submitting to authorities, and this wall symbolizes rejecting authority. Stand where you think you are when it comes to your parents. Do you submit completely? Do you reject completely? Or are you somewhere in the middle?" The preteens get up and stand where they think they are in their relationship with their parents. Then we say, "Okay, now think about where you'd like to be and slowly walk there. As you move, ask God for the power and wisdom to improve your relationship with your parents."
- We've split our teaching into shorter segments, with a chance for movement in between. We schedule worship throughout the lesson instead of all at the beginning. During moments where they're

singing, we invite preteens to come to the front of the room. Then, they go and sit down at chairs or couches. They get up again when it's time to go to their Small Groups. We have two Small Group times in our services—one at the beginning and one at the end. They're each around ten minutes long. A new leader once remarked how physically tired she was after the first night in our ministry because of all the movement.

- Sometimes, instead of opening service by singing a worship song, we'll use a song by a Christian artist and teach the preteens dance moves.
- Something we've learned from Patrick Snow is an activity called "Questions and Dancers." You give the preteens two possible answers to a question as part of a lesson. Both answers have a different dance move. "If you like Answer A, do this dance move when you hear the music. If you like Answer B, do this dance move when you hear the music."

These are just some examples of active learning strategies that involve physical responses.

WE'RE MORE LIKELY TO REMEMBER WHAT WE DO THAN WHAT WE SEE OR HEAR.

It's not surprising that active learning experiences are some of the most memorable teaching moments for preteens. Before our preteens move into youth ministry, we have a campfire and give them a chance to talk about their years in our ministry. We ask, "What is one of your most meaningful memories from Elevate?" Year after year, almost all of them will say one of these two things: a special event or a service that physically engaged them with the lesson.

Preteens love DOING, and it ministers to them.

We don't just talk about missions. We actually take our fourth and fifth graders on a one-day mission trip, and our sixth graders on a five-day mission trip. We don't just talk about serving the church. We have a leadership program where preteens are running the tech booth and leading worship and leading prayer and greeting and serving in other parts of the church. During a lesson about worship, preteens are given an opportunity to worship by creating. We set up nine tables, each with different media. We put on music and let preteens worship by creating something that glorifies God at the table of their choice. Then, they share what they created in their Small Groups.

In another series, we read 1 Peter 3:17 (NIV), which says, "For it is better, if it is God's will, to suffer for doing good than for doing evil." I could have followed up the reading of that passage by reading Paul's explanation of this found in 1 Peter 2:20. That would have produced low engagement and low retention of the lesson. Instead, I used an interactive learning strategy by saying the following.

"Paul tells us it's better to suffer for doing good than for doing evil. In your Small Groups, discuss this and put together a presentation to share with all of us in seven minutes. Why did Paul say this? Is he correct? Maybe Paul's wrong, and it isn't better to suffer for doing good than for doing evil. What do you think? Which is better? Why?"

Then, on a whiteboard, I wrote, "Do good and suffer, or do evil and suffer—which one is better?" I told the preteens that the group who presented the best reasoning for their answer was going to win a prize. The groups came up with some solid arguments for why it's better to do good and suffer. Then, we read 1 Peter 2:20 together to see what God's Word had to say about this. Of course, God's Word won the contest. This was a lesson that stuck.

Our preteens are not just hearers of the Word. They are doers.

IMPLEMENTING ACTIVE LEARNING TECHNIQUES OFTEN REQUIRES A SECOND PASS.

When I'm putting together a lesson for preteens, I'll create the content and know the main points I want to teach. In other words, I usually have a clear idea on the WHAT of a lesson. After I have a solid grasp on the WHAT, it's time for A Second Pass. With A Second Pass, I'm thinking of the lesson through the lens of HOW:

HOW will I teach the WHAT?

When I don't take A Second Pass, I often write lessons in which I expect preteens to sit in their chairs and absorb everything I'm speaking. When I perform A Second Pass, though, I think about the essentials we're exploring in this book. I ask myself, "Have I added components of movement, interaction, questions, and choices?"

When I focus only on the WHAT, I'm often left with a lecture instead of a lab. I'm left with preteens who didn't hear a word I said—preteens entirely disengaged from the living and active content of God's Word. But it's when I think about HOW that I truly invite them to be engaged in the learning process.

THERE'S AN INHERENT DANGER IN ACTIVE LEARNING METHODS.

It's possible to engage preteens in a lot of activity and have no learning come from the experience. The second half of the definition of active learning is just as important as the first: *"Instructional activities involving students in doing things **and thinking about what they're doing**."*

After preteens do something, they THINK about what they did. Thinking about what they did is critical because, without that, the activity might be of no benefit.

When I was in my twenties, I learned about something called the Experiential Learning Cycle. This concept, developed by David A. Kolb, was foundational in my understanding of how to best teach preteens. The Experiential Learning Cycle involves four steps, all of which are connected. Here they are, in order—but remember, it's a cycle. Step 1 follows Step 4. It's a never-ending sequence of continuing learning.

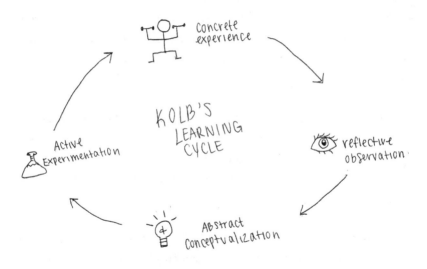

Step 1: Concrete Experience. These can be planned or naturally occurring experiences. You can develop a concrete activity for your preteens to experience (a game, a camp, an active learning experience within a lesson), or they may experience something you didn't plan. Perhaps, before a service starts, they have an experience that you can help them learn from.

Step 2: Reflective Observation. This often happens naturally after a concrete experience for adults; but for preteens, the right set of questions helps them think through their experience in a deeper way: "What happened?" or,

"How did you feel when that happened?" or, "What did you (or others) do in that experience?"

Step 3: Abstract Conceptualization. Whereas Step 2 involves looking backward and thinking through what happened, Step 3 involves looking forward and thinking through how the lesson learned will affect future behavior.

Step 4: Active Experimentation. In this step, a preteen is trying something out based on what he or she has learned from past experiences.

After our mission trip to San Francisco (Step 1), we plan a Sunday morning service where the preteens talk about what they experienced (Step 2). Then, they think about how the experience is going to affect them in the future (Step 3), and we challenge them to make their schools and neighborhoods their next mission trip (Step 4).

After we have the preteens play a game about generosity (Step 1), we ask them to think about how they acted during the game, and how their actions affected themselves and their group (Step 2). We then ask them to think about how they might play the game differently next time (Step 3), before giving them a chance to play again (Step 4).

The whole point here is that we don't just have preteens "DO," but we have them reflect on the things they've done and on what they're learning from what they're doing.

NOW...AN ACTIVE LEARNING OPPORTUNITY FOR YOU!

Here's the challenge:

Read through a lesson for preteens that's more like a lecture than a lab. Look for a section of the lesson that contains no activity or that is video- or teacher-driven. It might be a lesson you've written, or it might be a lesson from a curriculum you're using. After you've read through that section of the lesson and have a solid grasp on the WHAT being taught, take A Second Pass. Think about HOW you can change that section and make it a more active learning experience. You'll get bonus points if your idea involves physical activity.

If you don't have access to a lesson you can rewrite, start from scratch and develop an active learning activity that would help preteens learn something about Psalm 1. First, read the Psalm and think about WHAT you want to teach. Then, take A Second Pass and think of the HOW. Make sure to include an active learning experience.

If you're having difficulty thinking of ways to make a lesson more interactive, you might try Googling "interactive learning strategies." This will pull up a long list of articles containing a ton of ideas, like:

- Role-playing
- Question-and-answer forums
- Think-Pair-Share (give preteens a topic to think about on their own for a minute. Then, have them pair up and share their thoughts with a partner)
- Polls and Surveys
- Organizational Tasks (give preteens topics on strips of paper and have them organize the papers by topic or by true vs. false)
- ...and the list goes on and on and on. Just Google it. You'll have hours of active learning strategies to sort through

Remember, active learning means preteens do something and then think about what they did. For maximum impact, try to make it both interactive *and* physical.

I KNOW WHAT HAPPENS NEXT IF YOU'RE LIKE ME.

I've read books like this, in which the author is asking me to put the book down and do something. If you're like me, you'll want to move right on to the next chapter without doing the challenge activity described above.

As adults, we can move forward without completing an activity that will engage us in what we're learning, and we'll still get much of the value of the content we've just read. Because we've had years or even decades of life experience, we can, in our minds, draw from that well of experience to complete the experiential learning cycle in our minds without lifting a finger. We can recall experiences we've had and plug those into the learning cycle to make lessons gel in our minds.

However, preteens are different. They experience reality and learning in different ways because of their lack of life experience. For them, the value of doing a thing instead of just hearing about it cannot be overstated. Remember,

Preteens are ready developmentally, but not experientially.

An essential part of an Intentional Preteen Ministry is providing those experiences that will help preteens understand for themselves what a life of faith is like, instead of just telling them about it.

ESSENTIAL 6:
FACILITATE REFLECTION AND RESPONSE

There's an old video on YouTube called "Selective Attention Test." In it, two basketball teams (one wearing white shirts and one wearing black shirts) are simultaneously passing basketballs to their teammates while shuffling around in different directions. At the beginning of the video, a voice says, "This is a test of selective attention. Count how many times the players wearing white pass the basketball."

I've used this video as an intro game for our preteens. I'll have two contestants come to the front of the room and tell them, "Watch this video. This is going to be a contest to see who's paying attention."

At the end of the video, I ask an unexpected question: "What animal was in this video?"

Usually, the preteens don't know the answer. They didn't see any animal, because they were locked in on the basketball, counting the number of times it was passed by the team wearing white. What they didn't see was plain as day in a second viewing. In the midpoint of the video, somebody wearing a gorilla suit walks slowly into the middle of the circle of players passing the basketballs, beats on his or her chest, and then slowly walks out.

When we re-watch the video, the preteens think I've played some kind of trick on them—that the video they saw the first time was a different video than the one with the gorilla. But it's not.

This "selective attention" video is a variation on scientific research that points out something amazing about human beings: we don't really notice much of what's going on around us. We can't. There's so much information to process, and our brains are not wired to focus on everything at once. We must choose what to focus on, and everything else blurs into the background of our perception.

WHY DOES SELECTIVE ATTENTION HAPPEN?

In our minds are inhibitors, which help us focus on what's important. Psychotropic drugs interfere with these inhibitors, which is why people taking them lose their mind—all the information is coming in at once without being inhibited.

This world is incredibly intense and rich with information, and God has designed our brains to process reality by allowing us to be selective in our focus. By giving us the ability to select our focus, God has given us a way of glorifying Him.

WE NEED TO TAKE OUR MINDS CAPTIVE.

We aren't good at focusing on a lot of things, so we need to train our minds to focus on what's important. A big part of Intentional Preteen Ministry is helping preteens learn how to do the same.

As their minds are changing and their hormones are firing, the brain can become a jumbled mix of thoughts. A preteen allows his mind to shift focus from the mundane to the profound, from the immediate to the eternal, and from the important to the trivial. Sometimes, talking to a preteen can feel a bit like channel-surfing.

At the end of a recent service, I had a few pieces of fruit on the stage as part of an illustration. I felt great about the lesson—it seemed to me that I had communicated clearly and that my preteens had connected with the message. One boy remained standing at the edge of the teaching area after I had dismissed everyone to leave. In my mind, I thought, "He had a profound encounter with God tonight and wants to talk with me about what the service meant to him." It was just that sort of message. After I walked over to where he was, though, I was more than a little disappointed when he asked, "I was just wondering—can I have the apple?"

Preteens are like that.

Selective attention is a reality we all must face; and since preteens' thoughts tend to be all over the map from one second to the next, we need to help them learn how to actively choose a single destination to focus on. What is it that God wants all of us, including the preteens in our ministry, to place our attention on?

Is it other people? In certain ways, yes.

Is it God Himself? Absolutely.

Is it ourselves? Some people say, "No. God doesn't want us to focus on ourselves. He wants us to focus on others and on Him and forget about ourselves." I understand where that thought is coming from, but there are several Scriptures that indicate otherwise:

- "Pay close attention to yourself." (1 Timothy 4:16, NASB)
- "Think of yourself with sober judgment." (Romans 12:3, NIV)

- 2 Corinthians 13:5 says, "Examine yourself." It also says, "Test yourselves."

Throughout Scripture, we see God doing things like knocking Paul down and getting his attention. What does God do when He gets his attention? He helps Paul to see who He is, and at the same time, Paul realizes who *Paul* is. He goes by a new name, and his whole life gets bent in a new direction that honors God.

We see the same thing with Moses. Moses was about justice for the Israelites even before he fled to Midian. In fact, he was so passionate about justice that he committed murder when he encountered injustice in the way the Israelites were being treated by their slave masters. Justice was in Moses' heart, but it wasn't until Moses had his attention focused on who God was (in a burning bush) that God helped Moses to see who *Moses* was. It was after that personal encounter that God was able to take Moses' heart of justice and bend it towards a higher calling.

In the book *Strengthening the Soul of Your Leadership*, the author points out something I'd never noticed in the account of Moses in the wilderness. Think about what it says in Exodus 3:4 (NIV): "When the LORD saw that he had gone over to look, God called to him from within the bush." Moses had slowed down enough to pay attention to the right thing. When God saw Moses do that, THEN God spoke to him.

I know that, in ministry, I can get to the point where I'm focused on a variety of "important" things that I'm doing for the Lord, so much so that I don't take the time to examine myself. I don't take the time to sit still at Jesus' feet, focus my attention on Him, and pay attention to what He's saying about who I am. I don't take time to fulfill the Biblical mandate of testing myself and drawing out the purposes God has placed in my heart and mind.

An Intentional Preteen Ministry is one in which we train preteens to "turn aside and see" God. In this process, they'll learn how to see themselves as well.

IMAGINE FOR A MOMENT THAT YOU'RE WEARING A BACKPACK.

You wake up every day and put on this backpack, first thing. Inside the backpack are your thoughts, your emotions, where you're at in your relationships with God and with others, and the purposes of your heart.

If all you ever do is put this backpack on and go about your daily business, you might think you know what's going on inside of it, but you don't. If you don't stop and turn aside to look more closely, you don't really know what you're carrying around with you all day. You might miss seeing yourself in the hubbub of the day, just like you might miss seeing a gorilla in a basketball circle. Unless you stop to examine your life, how do you know what God is doing in it? *How do you know who God has made you to be?*

With preteens, this issue is amplified because they're changing so rapidly. It's as if somebody is stuffing their backpack full of new thoughts, new feelings, and new abilities every night while they sleep. Their backpacks can get full of new stuff, and they may not take even a moment during the day to look at what's inside. Preteens can be so focused on whatever their friends, teachers, and the media are directing their attention to that they end up having no idea what God is doing in them and through them.

One of the most valuable things we can do in an Intentional Preteen Ministry is create an environment in which preteens are given time to sit down and open their backpacks, and guided in how to do so.

We can help preteens learn how to create these kinds of moments for themselves throughout the week. We can teach them to pause each day and say, "God, I want to know You better. God, help me to know myself better. I can only focus my attention on so much, Lord. Help me to focus on what matters most to You." We have a unique opportunity in preteen ministry.

For the first time in their lives, preteens can think introspectively and see themselves in the third person. They couldn't do this when they were younger. There are two new things going on at once that complement one another:

1. Preteens have a lot of new things being added to their backpack.
2. Preteens are gaining the ability to think about what's in their backpack in ways they couldn't when they were younger.

Isn't God good? He doesn't just send us through a time of life when our backpack starts getting filled up; He sends us through this at the exact time in which we're finally able to start examining what's in our backpack. Reflection and response are, therefore, essential in the discipleship of preteens.

If all we do is teach, teach, and then teach some more, we're loading more stuff into their already-crowded backpacks without giving them time or space to examine what's already there. We're not giving them the essential opportunity to think about what's occupying their thought lives, and we're not giving them space to focus and grow like Moses did when he turned aside to see God, or like Paul did when he experienced those days of physical blindness, unable to see anything but what God was showing him.

DO YOU EVER WAKE UP AT 1 OR 2 AM?

Do you find yourself unable to sleep because your mind is buzzing with activity? In these moments, it might feel like God woke you up to talk with you and work through some things with you. This happens to me when I haven't set aside time for what I call "reflecting." Reflecting is summed up in the Bible verses bulleted earlier in the chapter—it's about being introspective; it involves prayer and silence as I examine myself and my life.

When I don't set aside time during the day to do the important work of reflecting, I wake up at 2 AM to do it. It's more restful for me when I schedule times of reflection into my week. Setting aside time for reflection is a tremendously helpful skill in our walk with the Lord, and we can teach this skill to the preteens in our ministries, too.

Developmentally, they're at a place where their backpack (their minds and their hearts) are being filled up with all sorts of new things...and they don't even know what those things are, because they haven't experienced them before! If we give them time during our services to think about and respond to the things God is showing them, we're instilling the practice of reflection.

IN AN INTENTIONAL PRETEEN MINISTRY, WE ANSWER THE QUESTION, HOW DO WE GIVE PRETEENS A CHANCE TO PROCESS WHAT THEY'RE LEARNING?

Even if I only had fifteen minutes in a service, I would build in times for reflection and give preteens a chance to respond to what they're learning.

That's how critical and valuable I find reflection and response to be. Here are six examples of how we've built reflection and response into our lessons.

1. Go to God

We'll set aside five minutes at the beginning of a service for preteens to go to God with old business before we teach anything new. After an opening worship song, I'll say, "Okay, before we get started with today's lesson, I want to give you a time to think about X."

X might be "how your day is going" or "a struggle that you've had this week at school." It could be anything that preteens might be carrying around that could take some time to unpack with God. Many times, we'll use the Go to God time as a review of what we talked about the prior week, and then we'll give them a chance to go to God with it: "Last week, we talked about fear and confidence. Before we start today's lesson, find a place around the room where you can sit and spend some talking with God about how you've been fearful or confident lately."

We've done this same activity at our summer camps: we'll give preteens time to sit somewhere by themselves and spend a little time with God. Sometimes, we'll even give them a journal or piece of paper where they can write down their thoughts. This is a chance for them to look into their backpacks and unpack them with God.

2. Mid-Message Pausing

When I'm teaching, I'll sometimes pause in the middle of a lesson. For example, I might say, "God is everywhere all at once. That's a mind-blowing thought. Let's pause and think for a minute about what it means that God is everywhere all at once."

During these mid-message pauses, it can be helpful to play some instrumental music while the preteens take a moment to reflect.

3. Reflection Questions

We've found that, when preteens get to Small Group, everybody wants to talk about random things; now, we'll give preteens reflection questions to think about BEFORE they go to Small Group.

I mentioned in Chapter 4 that we'll sometimes have everybody sit quietly and think about their answer to a question in Large Group. We may even have them write their answer down on a piece of paper. After they've had time to think, THEN we dismiss them to Small Groups. That way, they already have answers to the discussion questions and they're ready to discuss them.

Sending preteens to Small Group prepared to share has helped us have focused and productive Small Group times. It requires building in a few moments for silent reflection before dismissal to their groups, but it saves wasted time when they get there.

4. Writing

Writing is a great way to allow preteens to reflect. We invite them to write in response to a prompt:

- in journals
- on poster boards hung on a wall
- on index cards
- on unusual items that tie into the lesson, like a cinderblock or a pillow

Writing has the benefit of slowing your thinking—you can only write so fast. This can lead to more deliberate, "thoughtful" reflection.

5. Continuums

One time, we posted a long piece of butcher paper on the wall to create a continuum. We had "Don't Know About God" written at one end, "Know about

God" written in the middle, and "Know God" at the other end. There was a line between each of the sections.

In the lesson that day, we talked about the difference between knowing ABOUT God and knowing God, as we discussed Samuel's calling. As a way for the preteens to reflect, we gave them sticky notes. They wrote their names on the sticky notes and stuck them onto the continuum where they thought they were in their relationship with God. This allowed them to look inside their backpack and think about what they found. We made space for them to reflect on their relationship with God, and to publish their findings in a simple way.

We've done a similar continuum activity using shoes. Each preteen takes off one shoe in a Small Group circle and considers how closely they are following God this year. If they are following God as closely as possible, they put their shoe in the middle of the circle. The farther out they place their shoe, the less they are actively pursuing God. The discussion that comes out of these continuum reflection times is powerful. Many times, preteens are seeing truths about themselves for the first time. The truth has been tucked away in their backpack, and they didn't even know it was there until we gave them the space to do some soul-searching.

6. Response Stations

I mentioned in Chapter 4 that we give preteens time to respond at the end of messages. We set up different ways for them to do so, and let them choose which station they'll visit. Some stations involve writing. Some involve building. Some involve silence or music. Some involve talking or dancing.

Below are examples of response stations from a message about the love that The Everlasting God (*El Olam*) has for us. We taught the preteens about El Olam's love, but made sure to give them time to contemplate and reflect upon what God was showing them about Himself and His love for them.

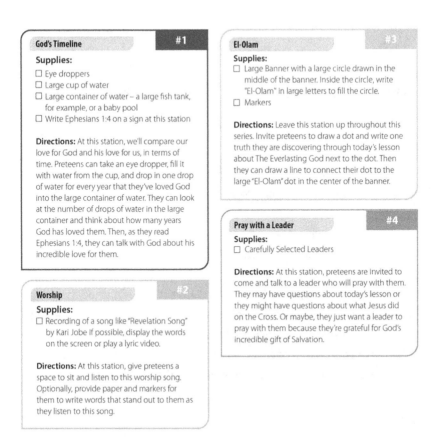

God's Timeline   #1

Supplies:
☐ Eye droppers
☐ Large cup of water
☐ Large container of water – a large fish tank, for example, or a baby pool
☐ Write Ephesians 1:4 on a sign at this station

Directions: At this station, we'll compare our love for God and his love for us, in terms of time. Preteens can take an eye dropper, fill it with water from the cup, and drop in one drop of water for every year that they've loved God into the large container of water. They can look at the number of drops of water in the large container and think about how many years God has loved them. Then, as they read Ephesians 1:4, they can talk with God about his incredible love for them.

Worship   #2

Supplies:
☐ Recording of a song like "Revelation Song" by Kari Jobe If possible, display the words on the screen or play a lyric video.

Directions: At this station, give preteens a space to sit and listen to this worship song. Optionally, provide paper and markers for them to write words that stand out to them as they listen to this song.

El-Olam   #3

Supplies:
☐ Large Banner with a large circle drawn in the middle of the banner. Inside the circle, write "El-Olam" in large letters to fill the circle.
☐ Markers

Directions: Leave this station up throughout this series. Invite preteens to draw a dot and write one truth they are discovering through today's lesson about The Everlasting God next to the dot. Then they can draw a line to connect their dot to the large "El-Olam" dot in the center of the banner.

Pray with a Leader   #4

Supplies:
☐ Carefully Selected Leaders

Directions: At this station, preteens are invited to come and talk to a leader who will pray with them. They may have questions about today's lesson or they might have questions about what Jesus did on the Cross. Or maybe, they just want a leader to pray with them because they're grateful for God's incredible gift of Salvation.

When it's time for Response Stations, we explain each station, set expectations for behavior, and then release the preteens to visit one or more station(s). After 5-10 minutes, we invite everybody to come to the front of the room and worship together as they finish whatever station they're at.

Giving preteens time to explore how they want to respond to a message helps them reflect upon what they've heard, rather than simply stuffing more information into their backpacks. This reflection time is when preteens move from knowing about God to taking steps of their own into a personal relationship with Him.

YOU MIGHT HAVE CONCERNS ABOUT THIS METHOD.

You might think that your preteens are going to be noisy, or that they're going to distract each other if you give them a moment to reflect during service. Just like we've learned with moments of active learning, these two things can help with times of reflection and response:

1. Set your expectations.
2. Reinforce your expectations.

Let your preteens know your expectations after you've explained a response activity, but before you release them to do it. Be clear. Then, make sure you and your other leaders are working to reinforce your expectations. As we've done these two things consistently, we've built a culture where most preteens engage with response activities without distracting others.

I KEEP A PHOTO OF A NOTE IN MY PHONE.

This is something a sixth-grade boy wrote a while back. We've addressed it as a church, but I've held on to the note as a reminder of the power of reflection and response time. Here's what he wrote during his reflection time:

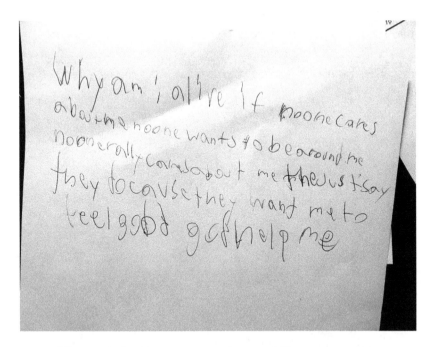

*"Why am I alive if no one cares about me? No one wants to be
around me. No one really cares about me. They just say they
do because they want me to feel good. God help me."*

If all I had done that day was teach and teach and teach and teach—if I hadn't
given this preteen time to reflect and write down his thoughts—we never
may have known what was going on inside of his "backpack." It's easy for me
to underestimate how much is going on in the heart and mind of a preteen. A
lot of times, I fall into the trap of thinking that I need to teach them a certain
amount of content, or else I haven't succeeded. Often, however, teaching
more is simply loading up their already-crammed backpacks.

Instead, I need to remember how powerful it is for preteens when I set aside
times throughout service for them to organize all of the confusing, new,
overwhelming, nebulous things that they're experiencing for the first time
in their lives. Sometimes, I even help them throw out a few things that don't
need to be in their backpacks at all.

Preteens are ready for deeper thinking and greater expressions of faith, but they have no experience in either of these things. Intentional Preteen Ministry creates a training ground in which preteens learn how to reflect and respond to the new things God is doing in them and through them.

ESSENTIAL 7:
DISCIPLE THROUGH QUESTIONS

Since we're going to explore the power of questions in this chapter, here's one for you to think about: *What do you see as a possible benefit of using questions in your ministry to preteens?*

Pause and contemplate that question until you come up with three answers. Perhaps you'll want to jot these answers down on a piece of paper or in the notes app on your phone. Take a moment and consider this question before you continue reading.

Okay. Now that you've paused and thought through the question, here's another: *In what ways did pausing and thinking about that last question change your engagement level with the content being presented in this book?*

Isn't it interesting? Questions can instantly change our engagement level and experience. Asking questions has been a common Rabbinical technique for drawing people deeper into a discussion for centuries. Jesus asked over three hundred questions in the Gospels. Why? Because they're essential in the process of discipleship.

As we strive to help preteens in the development of their faith, questions can be one of our most powerful tools. Let's look at four reasons why.

1. Questions help preteens verbalize what they think.

Preteens are at an interesting age. They're having a myriad of experiences and feelings that are new to them. Often, they don't have language to put to their feelings and experiences. It's the first time they've felt betrayed by a friend. It's the first time they're thinking abstract thoughts and under-standing analogies in a deeper way. It's the first time they realize certain things about their parents as human beings.

When you ask preteens questions, you're inviting them to verbalize what they may have never spoken before. You may ask a question like, "When was a time you felt weak?" When you do that, there may be preteens who verbalize something for the first time. These new thoughts and feelings are forming inside their minds and hearts; asking effective questions will give them chances to speak those thoughts and feelings out loud.

Questions can help preteens to formulate their thoughts and feelings better and, ultimately, to understand themselves better.

2. Questions demonstrate that preteens have value.

When we ask questions, we're inviting preteens to engage with the Church. They aren't just coming to a show. They aren't just coming to hear how smart we are. When we ask them questions, preteens get the sense that they are an integral part of what's happening. We are sending the message, "You're a part of this. Your thoughts matter. We care about you and what you think."

3. Questions draw preteens into the process.

Not only do questions SHOW that you care about the preteens being involved in the process; questions DO involve the preteens in the process. Questions help preteens to have control and to partake in the learning experience in a more active and engaging way than passively listening while the teacher does all of the "work."

4. Questions are more likely to hold a preteen's interest than statements.

Imagine you're speaking to a group of preteens, and you perform an illustration to help explore a Bible verse displayed on the screen. How would you help preteens make the connection between the illustration and the verse?

Option 1: "Let me tell you how this illustration demonstrates the truth of the Bible verse on the screen," followed by an explanation.

Option 2: "Who can tell me how this illustration is like this Bible verse on the screen?"

In Option 1, the preteens are passive. They may look engaged, but there's really no way of knowing if they're making the connection you were hoping they'd make. In Option 2, they're actively engaged in the process. Even if they all don't raise their hand to give an answer, you've invited them into a much deeper place of engagement than if you'd just told them the answer.

Those are four benefits of using questions. I'm sure you could think of even more. Questions are powerful tools that Jesus, our supreme example, used often. So, what's stopping us from using more questions?

WHAT IS STOPPING US FROM USING THIS POWERFUL DISCIPLESHIP TOOL TO HELP OUR PRETEENS TAKE OWNERSHIP OF THEIR FAITH?

Here are 5 reasons why I'm not prone to ask preteens questions as a ministry leader.

1. **I wasn't trained in how to use questions.** My education was focused on how to find the answers I should give, not the questions I should ask.

2. **I've been told that the power of leadership comes in having good answers, not good questions.** This is an incorrect mindset, and that's become clearer to me as I've considered Jesus' example. Power in leadership is often found in asking good questions, not in having the answers.

3. **I'm not accustomed to this type of leadership.** In my life, leaders haven't typically asked me a lot of questions. They've led in other ways, which has caused me to NOT equate leading with asking. There was one exception to this rule, and that was my teachers in school. They asked me plenty of questions—mostly on tests. By and large, though, my teachers tended to ask just one question, although it may have taken the form of 50 different questions on a test. The one question they were asking me over and over was, "Did you learn what I wanted you to learn?"

4. **I want to appear to know my stuff.** If a preteen asks a question in Small Group, I don't want him to think I don't know the answer, especially if *I know* that I know the answer. A preteen might ask, "Did Jesus have to die on the cross?" What's my first instinct? To share with him or her what I know, of course. I want to appear to have the knowledge. Think of how differently a preteen would be engaged, though, if they ask a question and I respond with, "Well, what do you think?" Or, "Does anybody else know?" Letting go of the bike in this way requires swallowing our pride.

5. **I'm in a hurry.** Questions take more time. When I ask a question, I must make space and time for the answer, and give up control of how long each portion of a service is going to take. I don't know how long it's going to take for the preteen I called on to answer a question—or if their answer is going to take the discussion in an

unexpected direction. If I DON'T ask questions, I can give the answers myself and control the timing of each segment of service. I can make the point quickly and BAM, move on to the next thing. Failing to ask questions may seem efficient, but it doesn't lend itself to transformative teaching, does it?

Pause for a moment and think about this question: *How could you have used a question to enhance a recent teaching moment with preteens?*

Maybe there's a specific moment you can think of in a Small Group or Large Group setting in which you could have asked a question instead of giving an answer. Mark your spot in the book and ponder this question. When you come back, we'll consider six types of questions that we can ask preteens.

BLOOM'S TAXONOMY WAS CREATED IN 1956 UNDER THE LEADERSHIP OF EDUCATIONAL PSYCHOLOGIST DR. BENJAMIN BLOOM.

It was revised in 2001. Bloom looked at the types of questions that can be asked and divided them into six different levels of cognitive complexity.

BLOOM'S TAXONOMY

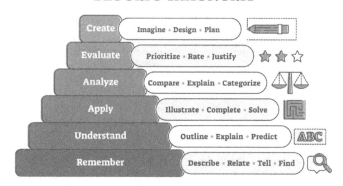

It's helpful to think of Bloom's Taxonomy like a musical instrument—like a 6-string guitar. The goal of an intentional ministry leader is not to get to the highest level of complexity every time when asking questions. Instead, in order to create the most beautiful music within ministry, we should attempt to use *all* the strings.

Let's briefly survey and discuss all six levels of questions. For the purposes of this book, we'll stick to a basic description of Bloom's Taxonomy; but if it captures your interest, there is a plethora of resources on this topic.

Level 1: Knowledge (Remember)

These questions ask preteens to identify information in the same form in which it's presented.

Knowledge-based questions are the standard on school tests. You're taught that George Washington was married in 1759. The question on the test is, "In what year was George Washington married?" Google and Siri are best equipped to answer these types of questions because they require the simple regurgitation of facts.

Until recently, school teachers tended to use this type of question almost exclusively. According to Anthony D. Fredericks in his 2010 book, *The Teacher's Handbook*, observations of elementary and secondary classrooms have shown that many teachers will ask upward of 300 or more knowledge-based questions in a day.[6]

We use knowledge-based questions in church, too. We want to make sure that preteens know and understand the facts of the Bible.

Here are some examples:

- What are the first five books of the Bible?
- Who was David's son?
- What does Isaiah 41:10 say?

Knowledge questions are typically regurgitation of the material that has been taught.

Level 2: Comprehension (Understand)

With comprehension questions, you're taking different pieces of information you've heard and combining them into one comprehensive thought.

Let's say you're reading Luke chapter 15 with a group of preteens. In that chapter, Jesus tells stories about the lost coin, the lost sheep, and the lost son. After reading this chapter, you ask a comprehension question:

- What do these three stories have in common?
- What is the connection between these three stories?

Comprehension questions are all about taking different pieces of information and combining them into one cohesive truth.

Here are some other examples of comprehension questions:

---

6   Fredericks, Anthony D. *The Teacher's Handbook: Strategies for Success*. R&L Education. January 16, 2010.

- What did David do every time he had a chance to harm King Saul?
- Can you use your own words to explain the point of the story we just read?

Comprehension questions can help you find out if a preteen understands something well enough to combine it with other truths.

Level 3: Application (Apply)

These questions are all about applying truths to new situations. They ask, "How does what you learn affect the way you live?" Application questions are often the most difficult for preteens to answer. I don't exactly know why this is, but I've seen it over and over in my experience with them. Perhaps it has to do with their lack of life experience and the limited amount of time they've had the ability to see themselves in the third person.

I've worded application questions in several different ways to preteens, but they always seem to struggle with this type of thinking. It's difficult for them to take a bit of knowledge and apply it to a situation in their lives. Being specific in application questions seems to help. Asking a question like, "Because God gives you strength, what's something you can do this week?" is harder for a preteen to answer than more specific questions, such as these:

- How can the fact that God gives you strength help you when you're lying in bed at night, scared?
- How does knowing that God is always with you make a difference in the way you act at school during a difficult test?

One method I've discovered that helps preteens with application is found in a two-letter word:

SO

During service, I'll have preteens write down one truth they heard during the lesson that they don't want to forget. After giving them a moment to do this, I'll say, "Now, at the end of the truth you wrote, add the word 'SO.' Then, finish the statement. For example, if you wrote

'Music has the power to affect my mood'

as your truth, your full statement might be,

*'Music has the power has the power to affect my mood, **SO** I'll be more careful about the music I choose to listen to.'"*

The word "SO" has amazed me with its potential to help preteens step into application. That little word seems to be one of the most effective application "questions" I can ask a preteen.

Over the years, I've become far more interested in preteens experiencing transformation than application. **Application** is a mental process in which we usually invite somebody to mentally apply a truth to one imagined situation. **Transformation** is more than just a mental activity; it's holistic. If a preteen is transformed by a truth, it affects the way she acts in *all* situations.

Application questions—even questions like "SO...?"—can be helpful, though. When preteens answer an application question, they envision what it will look like when they are transformed by Jesus in that area.

Level 4: Analysis (Analyze)

Analysis means that you're breaking something down into parts to understand it. At this level, a preteen takes apart a big idea or story into smaller pieces in order to look at each one of them.

Just like "So?" is a great example of an application question, "Why?" is a great example of an analysis question:

- Why did Jesus die on the Cross?
- Why did Saul attack David?
- Why does God say, "Do not fear" so often in Scripture?

Analysis is an invitation to investigate a situation without being told ahead of time how all the parts of that situation work.

Level 5: Evaluation (Evaluate)

Evaluation is making a judgment about something:

- What do you think about how David treated King Saul?
- Do you think it's valuable for people to memorize Scripture?
- How do you feel when you worship God?

Like synthesis, these questions yield answers unique to the individuals who are answering. You're asking them to put a value on something. When you ask preteens these types of questions, you're inviting them to share their opinions—to think about the actions they want to choose for their lives.

Level 6: Synthesis (Create)

This is my favorite kind of question to ask preteens. If I "over-ask" one type of question, this is the one. Synthesis questions ask preteens for creative and original thought.

Here are some examples:

- What do you think would happen if David had attacked King Saul when he had the chance?
- Take all the first letters of words that represent big fears in your life. Take those letters and make a name out of it.
- Read Psalm 100. If there were three more lines added to the end of this Psalm, what might they say?

Each person can generate a unique answer to a synthesis question, and each answer is just as "correct." One of my favorite things about working with preteens is their ability to engage in this type of thinking in ways they couldn't when they were even six months younger. Synthesis questions allow preteens to spread some of those "new wings" of higher-level thinking that they're starting to develop. Synthesis questions allow them to flex their new "explore the possibilities" muscles.

WITH THE KNOWLEDGE OF BLOOM'S TAXONOMY IN THE BACK OF YOUR MIND, YOU CAN ASK BETTER QUESTIONS OF YOUR PRETEENS.

Used effectively, these questions can help us let go and run beside our preteens as they take ownership of their faith walks. If you're asking the same level of questions over and over, you may be missing an opportunity to engage a preteen in spiritual growth at a deeper level.

After reading this information, you might challenge yourself to ask three synthesis questions this week, or to look through the questions you have in an upcoming lesson and ensure that you have a variety of question types included. If you use different types of questions to broaden your Small Group and Large Group discussions, you'll start to unleash the power of questions with preteens.

Let's pause for a moment and consider how this might work. Doing this will help cement the concepts of this chapter into your long-term memory.

1. Imagine that you've just read the account of Noah building the ark with a group of preteens.
2. Grab a sheet of paper or open the notes app in your phone.

3. Write down six questions you could ask a group of preteens, making sure that these questions represent each of the levels in Bloom's Taxonomy.
4. Note which questions would most likely help your preteens to take ownership of their faith.

QUESTIONS ARE HELPFUL FOR EFFECTIVE DISCIPLINE, TOO.

In this chapter, we've focused primarily on using questions as a teaching technique; but questions can also play an important role as we discipline preteens.

First, let's distinguish between discipline and punishment.

Discipline is about building up. **Punishment** is about making small.

Discipline comes from the same root as disciple. **Punishment** comes from the same root as puny.

To **discipline** is to teach; to **punish** is to inflict harm or to make somebody conform to the way you want them to act.

One is child-centered and the other is leader-centered.

Over the years, I've worked with many preteens who have various discipline issues. Sometimes, I've felt like a complete failure in helping a preteen to overcome negative behavior, and I was happy when the preteen with persistent behavior issues finally moved on to the next class. However, there have been times we've seen amazing changes in a struggling preteen, and we know that our ministry team had a hand in discipling them.

I think of Carlos. On his first day at our church—within ten minutes of meeting him—Carlos said to me, "You'll probably kick me out. That's what they did at the last church we were at." True story. It didn't take long to see why they kicked him out, either. He could have won a gold medal in defiance and troublemaking.

However, our ministry team surrounded Carlos with loving discipleship. Fifteen months later, Carlos was a valuable part of our student leadership team. Asking questions was a big part of our discipline strategy with Carlos.

WHERE DO WE START WHEN DISCIPLINING A PRETEEN?

The most effective discipline for preteens seems to take place when we go on a mental and emotional walk with them down the path they're currently on. Then, we can use questions to gently guide them toward a path that is bent toward Jesus—a path that will ultimately be better for them, because it leads to fullness of life.

Here are four key questions we can ask ourselves that will cause us to "run beside" misbehaving preteens *before* we begin to help them correct their paths.

Question 1: "Is this a good time?" (Ephesians 6:4; Ecclesiastes 3:7)

In a moment of passion, a preteen may experience something called "amygdala hijack." The amygdala is a part of the brain that regulates emotions, and it can be so supercharged in a heated moment of misbehavior that it makes it physically impossible for the preteen to use the logic center of the brain. It's useless to reason with a preteen when the emotion center has hijacked his or her entire brain.

If we're going to walk with a preteen and help disciple him or her toward a better path, sometimes we will need to deal with the troubling behavior "at a later time" instead of "in the moment." We might need to revisit the behavior the following Sunday before service, or sometime during the week in a non-confrontational setting (like an ice cream shop). There is wisdom in giving a preteen time to "cool off" before you attempt to discuss things. This doesn't mean we don't address issues; it simply means we choose a time to do so that will likely be fruitful.

Question 2: "Why are they acting this way?" (1 Samuel 16:7)

If you want to speak truth to a preteen that he or she will receive, start by showing interest in that preteen's motivations. Interest proceeds entrance.

When I see a misbehavior, it's not helpful to simply think, "That preteen is doing such-and-such, and I want him/her to stop now! How do I get him/her to stop?" This type of thinking tends to lead me toward punishment techniques rather than discipline techniques. What helps me walk alongside the misbehaving preteen, instead, is to become curious about why he or she is demonstrating those behaviors. What's the story behind the actions I'm seeing? What's the motivation? I ask myself questions and really get curious about the thinking and emotion behind the behavior.

When you see an iceberg floating above the ocean, you're only seeing ten percent of the entire iceberg. The BEHAVIOR is just the visible tip of iceberg, but what I need to understand is the ninety percent—the MOTIVATION that lies beneath the surface.

If I can become curious about what preteens are trying to accomplish or communicate with their behavior, and if I ask myself some questions about it, I can start to understand their motivations.

When his grandma started bringing him to our preteen ministry, Joe seemed sad and antisocial. His behaviors weren't typical for a fifth-grade boy. He was a special kind of rude and defiant. I noticed Joe's behavior, but didn't know what was beneath the surface. One day, in Small Group, he finally explained that his dad was an alcoholic and his mom had died. That's why he had gone to live with Grandma. There was so much going on beneath the surface. There usually is with a kid like Joe.

Question 3: "How can I walk alongside this preteen?" (Ecclesiastes 4:9-10)

Let's say I have a preteen named Bella, and I'm talking with her to better understand her motivations: "Bella, can you tell me what you were trying to accomplish by acting that way?" In my own head, I'm wondering the same thing: "What was she trying to accomplish?"

As I'm listening to her response, I'm comparing her answers with what I thought they would be; if there's a difference, I know I need to ask another question because I'm not thinking in the same way that Bella is. Instead of trying to get Bella to think my way—or God's way, or "the correct way"—about a situation, I approach the situation with the goal of first understanding Bella's way of thinking. As I ask more questions and listen, there becomes more and more similarities between her answers and the ones I'm imagining. Now, we're walking down this path together. Bella will begin to sense that she's not alone in her journey.

There have been so many times when preteens have answered questions that I've asked about their behavior, and I either didn't believe them or understand what they meant. Instead of truly considering what they were trying to convey and affirming their answers, I've dismissed them. When I dismiss what they're saying as dumb or untrue, we go in different directions. I'm not walking alongside them on their journey. Remember, this is THEIR journey. It's counterproductive to the goal of discipline to dismiss or belittle the journey they're on. How can we come together in understanding what needs to happen next if we aren't walking together?

If I'm dismissing them, I'm missing them.

Instead of dismissing, I do well to pause and consider their answers. I do well to affirm their answers by repeating back to them what they're telling me. I do well to give them the benefit of the doubt and believe the best in them. The more I do this, the more I find that preteens trust me with the deeper truths behind their actions, and the more I can start to really under-stand them. Remember, interest proceeds entrance.

Question 4: "What do I not understand about the situation?" (James 1:19)

Sometimes, preteens will know that what they're doing is wrong, and they're just waiting to get caught and yelled at. If we start asking them questions about their behavior, and if we honestly want to understand the situation better, it can be really disarming for them.

Honest questions can disarm a preteen who's misbehaving by helping them think, "Okay, here's somebody who's on my side. They want to be on my side. They want to understand why I'm doing what I'm doing. I'm not alone in what I'm trying to accomplish. I can bring somebody else into this journey I'm on."

Dishonest questions can do the opposite—they can escalate a situation. These are questions like "What are you doing?!? Why are you doing that?!? What's wrong with you?!?" Those aren't honest questions. Those are accu-sations disguised as questions. An honest question is one that you ask when you're honestly seeking information from the misbehaving preteen.

NOW THAT WE'RE WALKING SIDE-BY-SIDE WITH A STRUGGLING PRETEEN AND DISCIPLING HIM, WE CAN ASK QUESTIONS TO HELP HIM TAKE OWNERSHIP OF HIS FUTURE.

Here are a few types of questions we can ask:

REFLECTIVE

These questions help preteens understand themselves. Reflective questions like, "Why are you acting like that?" asked in a non-confrontational way can help preteens consider what they're doing and what they're trying to accomplish.

Here are a couple examples of reflective questions:

- "How were you feeling when you did that?"
- "What did you think was going to happen when you did that?"
- "Did you think it was okay for you to do that? No? Oh, okay. Well, why'd you do it then?"

These types of reflective questions, asked in a gentle tone, can help preteens look at themselves, consider the situations they're in, and then self-report. They're evaluating themselves. They may not have asked themselves these questions. They might not have thought about why they're doing what they're doing.

Sometimes, preteens may answer reflective questions, especially if they're feeling defensive, by saying, "I DON'T KNOW!" Guess what? That might be the truth. They might not know why they did what they did; but with gentle, honest questions and guidance from the Holy Spirit, you can help them see some truths about themselves. This approach is so useful for preteens, who are just now gaining the ability to see themselves in the third person.

CONSEQUENTIAL

Sometimes, preteens don't evaluate the consequences of their actions. Asking questions about consequences can help preteens begin to think in that way. Here are some examples:

- "Did you see what happened after you did that?"
- "Did you see how people reacted?"

- "What's going to happen now that you did that?"
- "What happens when people [steal]?"

Often, preteens more easily understand the effects of an action, and identify those effects, when the question is not initially tied to them. Think of David, when he had committed adultery with Bathsheba. The prophet Nathan started by telling a story about somebody else and asking David questions about that figure. Then, and only then, Nathan said, "You are the man."

When disciplining preteens, we can use a similar approach to help them see the consequences of their actions. Start by asking more generalized questions about stealing or whatever the troubling behavior was. Then, and only then, ask them to make the connection to their own behavior.

UNDERSTANDING THE PROBLEM

Sometimes, preteens may not even understand why their behaviors are a problem: "I don't see why it's a problem for me to ride on somebody's shoulders while he runs around the sanctuary!"

We can help preteens think objectively about their behaviors by asking more generalized questions that are aimed at helping them understand why their behavior is a problem:

- "Do you understand why lying is a problem?"
- "Do you want people to lie to you? Why not?"
- "Why do you think God instructs us not to lie?"
- "What do you think would happen if everybody lied?"

Remember, this needs to be honest questioning, in which you're seeking their thoughts rather than making an accusation. You can easily ask this type of question in an escalating way: "WHAT DO YOU THINK WOULD HAPPEN IF EVERYBODY LIED?!"

Instead, use this type of question to honestly engage preteens in conversation and get them to think through their behaviors for themselves.

FUTURE PLANNING

You could simply tell a preteen, "Hey, next time you're angry, do this," or, "Next time you want something that isn't yours, do this." However, we know that questions are more engaging because they allow preteens to OWN their answers.

You can turn your solution into a question. This becomes an invitation for preteens to solve the dilemma they're facing themselves:

- "What else could you have done in that situation?"
- "What could you do the next time that happens?"
- "If you want to have friends, what would be a better way for you to act?"

WHEN YOU USE QUESTIONS IN DISCIPLINE SITUATIONS, YOU'RE ENGAGING PRETEENS AND SHOWING THEM THAT YOU WANT TO WALK BESIDE THEM AND HELP THEM ON THEIR PATHS.

By asking questions, you can create unity between you and your preteens who have behavior issues. Then, you'll be able to help them correct their paths themselves and walk in new and better ways.

Pause for a moment. Grab a piece of paper or open to your phone's notes app. Think about this question: *What is one difficult behavior issue you've seen in a student, and how might you use questions to discipline that student?*

Is there a preteen in your ministry who drives you crazy? Is there a behavior from a preteen that you can't seem to stop? Think about this and consider what honest questions you could ask to help discipline, rather than punish, that individual.

QUESTIONS ACTIVATE FAITH!

Questions, used wisely, have the power to help preteens in their walk with Christ. Questions engage preteens and put the control into their hands.

Preteens are at an age where their faith starts to become their own. It's no longer their parents' faith that they're simply emulating; it's THEIR faith. Questions can play a critical role in this process. We ask preteens questions to get them to think about what they truly believe, as well as to say what they think and feel. Questions help them self-reflect and correct the paths they're on.

Preteens are breaking out of, "Mom says this, so it's this." "Santa exists because my parents say so." They are in the beginning phase of breaking out of their reliance on others. They are starting to think of deeper questions for the first time:

- "Is God real?"
- "If Jesus already forgave my sins, why shouldn't I sin as much as I want?"
- "Could the things I'm reading in the Bible really have happened?"

4th-6th graders are exploring possibilities. As we ask questions, we help them explore in a safe environment. Two of the most powerful questions we've found to ask preteens during a ministry event or service are these:

"What is God showing you today?"

"What questions do you have?"

These questions are powerful, because they directly connect the preteen with what's been presented in the event or service. These questions get at the heart of what they think about what you've taught. Their answers help us understand their relationship with Christ, as well as giving us a glimpse of how to best proceed as we minister to them. Asking these questions consistently encourages preteens to listen for what God might be speaking to them during a service. It gives them permission to question what they believe about God and to wrestle with the true nature of their developing faith.

I heard this statement, and it's worth considering: "Doubt is not the opposite of faith, it's the environment for faith."

Faith isn't something we'll need in Heaven. In 2 Corinthians 13, it talks about faith, hope, and love, and says that love is the only one that remains. When we're in Heaven, we won't need hope anymore, because we'll be in the place we've hoped for. We won't need faith anymore, because we'll see everything clearly. Faith only exists now because of doubt. Hebrews 11:1 (ESV) says, "Faith is the assurance of things hoped for, the conviction of things not seen."

Asking difficult questions of preteens, and allowing them to ask difficult questions—even questions coming from a place of doubt—can create an environment in which faith is developed instead of just discussed.

QUESTIONS FACILITATE CORRECTION.

As they are moving towards a greater faith in God, preteens will likely have thoughts about God that are untrue. We can use questions to draw those thoughts out of their brains and then, because we know what they're thinking, we can also use questions to help preteens see the flaws in their thinking for themselves.

If a preteen said something incorrect about God, I can simply say, "No, you're wrong. Here's the truth..." If I do that, he might not accept my conclusion; he certainly won't own the answer to the same degree that he would have if he'd reached the conclusion on his own. However, if I ask preteens questions about a misconception they have, I can help them come to a correct conclusion. This is much more powerful than me telling them what they should think.

We all know this. It's far more powerful to discover a truth ourselves than to have somebody tell us that truth. The biggest "Aha!" moments in my life weren't when a teacher said something and I said, "Yes!" The biggest "Aha!" moments in my life were those in which I finally connected the dots myself! When we ask questions, we give preteens the opportunity to connect those dots and create for themselves powerful "Aha!" moments.

Questions are so powerful; Jesus used them over and over. As you finish this chapter, pause and look at one example of Jesus' use of questions. In Mark 8:1-29, Jesus asks around ten questions. Take a moment and analyze why Jesus asks these questions. This is where we'll end this chapter, with a question:

What was Jesus up to with all those questions in Mark 8?

ESSENTIAL 8:
BUILD A FOUNDATION FOR IDENTITY FORMATION

mall Group leaders who work with nine-year-olds in our ministry have remarked that identity isn't as compelling a topic for them. This is especially true, I've found, for the boys' groups. Discussion questions about identity do little to engage them. However, leaders who work with sixth graders—and especially with girls (who tend to mature more quickly than boys)—tell me that issues of identity are of great importance to them, and that questions about identity typically generate a lot of discussion.

As preteens mature, identity becomes more of a central issue. Think about a two-year-old child. He'll dance in front of a crowd of any size without reservation or concern about how people perceive him. That child at twelve years old might have anxiety about the exact same activity. What's changed?

Preteens develop the ability to see themselves in the third person, and they start paying attention to the fact that others are noticing and thinking about them. It's part of God's good plan that we become aware of ourselves and start wondering about our identity. The preteen years are when kids take their first steps toward understanding their identity. It's when they're first able to consider who they are and how they are perceived by others.

What an amazing opportunity we have! If we're intentionally ministering to preteens, we are cognizant that they're just starting to ask the question, "Who am I?" As they're do this, we can point them to God's answers from Scripture during a tiny window of time in which the foundations of identity are being built. This is yet another reason why an Intentional Preteen Ministry can be so impactful.

Jane Kroger, in her book *Identity Development*, writes this about fifth through eighth graders: "The biological changes of puberty, the move to more complex ways of thinking, redefining the self within the family, developing new forms of relationship with peers and adapting to the more complex demands of a junior high or middle school, all raise important identity considerations for the young adolescent."[7]

A lot of factors contribute to the development of identity. You might say, "Well, we only work with fifth graders. They're not in middle school yet." Still, most fifth graders are dealing with at least four of the things Jane Kroger mentions. They are in the beginning stages of asking questions about their own identity. Just like everything else we do with preteens, the answer isn't simply to tell them who they are in Christ, but to let go of the bike and run beside as they discover this for themselves.

Let's look at four ways in which preteens try to answer the question, "Who am I?" and how we can run beside them in these beginning stages of identity formation.

WAY 1: TRIAL AND ERROR

The trial and error process gives preteens a chance to try on different identities and see how they fit. You might be seeing trial and error when a preteen

7   Kroger, Jane. *Identity Development: Adolescence Through Adulthood (Achieving QTLS Series).* SAGE Publications, Inc. July 11, 2006.

acts like the star of the show one week, but the next week is off in the corner acting shy; or when the sixth grader who is super helpful and super kind suddenly becomes sarcastic and rude. This behavior can confound ministry leaders and parents, but often it's just a preteen experimenting with the possibilities, trying out different identities to see how they fit.

It's important to keep an eye on sudden changes, because it might be a sign of something more serious, like abuse or drug use. In many cases, however, changes in personality expression are a sign that a preteen is on a journey to discovering his or her identity.

How do we partner with this approach? As we work with preteens who are trying on identities like they're clothes, we can remember the importance of power and choice. We begin by affirming that they can, in fact, try things out. That is within their power.

Then, we can help them go beyond simply doing things because it's within their power. We can point them to the truths of Scripture, which help them think more critically about their decisions. There are verses like, "Whether you eat or drink or whatever you do, do it all for the glory of God" (1 Corinthians 10:31, NIV), and, "You say, 'I am allowed to do anything'—but not everything is good for you. You say, 'I am allowed to do anything'—but not everything is beneficial" (1 Corinthians 10:23, NLT).

By asking preteens to think about their actions and attitudes and whether these fulfill God's design and desire for them—to glorify Him and to build others up—we give preteens a matrix with which to evaluate their expressions of self. We can help preteens move from a place where they're thinking, "I'm going to make choices and they're going to be mine," to a place where they start thinking, "Yes, this is my choice...but is it a good choice?"

As leaders, another way we can partner with preteens is by having realistic expectations. We should expect inconsistent behavior and personality from early adolescents. The same kid who is a leader one week may be a follower the next week, and that's okay. It's part of the process. I also shouldn't paint preteens into a corner with my expectations. When I give space for preteens to try out new identity expressions, I'm giving them opportunities to find their true, God-given identities.

A few years back, there was a boy in our preteen ministry who was a special kind of trouble. He was a kid who had been known to cause problems before check-in even started. His parents didn't bring him and yet, each week, he found a way to get to our ministry. What happened with Cole, over time, was that we gave him space to assume a new identity. The leaders did an amazing job of not painting him into a corner; never did I hear them say, "Oh no. There's Cole again."

Occasionally, Cole—like almost all preteens I've ever met—tried something outside his regular M.O. When he did, our leaders noticed and made mention of it. "Cole, you're letting God change your heart, aren't you? That's so awesome to see." Over time, Cole discovered that he was a kid whom Jesus loved, and someone who was designed to bring his Best Friend glory just by being himself.

Before you continue reading, stop for a moment and read the account in Mark 10: 46-52. It describes Jesus' encounter with blind Bartimaeus. As you read it, notice where Bartimaeus is, physically, at the beginning of the story, and notice where he is, physically, at the end of the story. Also notice how people perceive and respond to Bartimaeus, and contrast that with how Jesus perceives and responds to Bartimaeus.

Isn't it interesting? In verse 46 of Mark 10, it says that Bartimaeus was sitting *by the road.* By verse 52, it says he's following Jesus *along the road.*

In verse 48, it says that the other people who were with Jesus rebuked Bartimaeus and told him to be quiet. Why? because they were seeing Bartimaeus as he was portraying himself to be. Jesus, however, saw his full potential and his true identity. Jesus saw Bartimaeus not as a worthless beggar, but as a beloved disciple.

As our preteens are trying out different identities—as they come each week and flip-flop from being this kind of person to that kind of person—I pray that we have eyes like Jesus and that we don't just say to misbehaving preteens, "Go sit back down where you were."

I don't always get this right. I've sent a preteen out of the room without any desire to see him repent or step into his true identity in Christ. It turns out that I'm the one who has needed to repent at times. Other times, I do get it right, and I say to a misbehaving preteen, "I see potential in you. I see the potential that Christ sees in you."

There are many verses we like to read because they make us feel good about who we are in Christ. We are Christ's workmanship. We are a royal priesthood. We are forgiven. We are children of God. We are friends of God. As I read these verses, I need to remind myself that these identity statements aren't just true for me—they're also true for preteens who, for the first time in their lives, are trying to figure out who they are.

Instead of painting them into a corner, I can give them a chance to try different things. I can give them systems for evaluating their choices, and I can help them step into an identity that, like Bartimaeus, will help them get off of the side of the road and get them walking on the road with Jesus.

Here, then, is my prayer: "Help me, God, to see them with your eyes."

WAY 2: IMITATION

A second approach preteens take to solving their "Who am I?" question is to imitate others. They might imitate a peer. They might imitate an adult they respect. They might imitate somebody famous. They might even imitate you.

Have you ever seen a fourth grader show up for church wearing a big old bow in her hair, just like a famous person she likes? This may be part of her attempt to figure out her identity. She's trying to answer the question, "Who am I?" by copying somebody who she admires. Likewise, you might have a twelve-year old boy who comes to church with a certain hairdo or dressed a certain way—a carbon copy of one of the leaders in your ministry.

I was talking to my tenth-grade daughter as I prepared to write this. I asked her, "How do you think preteens try to figure out their identity?" She talked about how she tried imitating different things that she saw in others. She could remember that there were certain things about Taylor Swift and Hollyn that she liked. She remembers consciously dressing like them a little bit, wearing her hair like them, and even talking like them.

You might see this same thing in your ministry: preteens imitating other people as they figure out their own identities.

How do we partner with this approach? Here's a quote from the AMLE: "Young adolescents tend to emulate their esteemed peers and non-parent adults." This is great to know, because that second part—the "non-parent adults" part—indicates that we ministry leaders have an important part to play in the development of preteens' identities.

In 1 Corinthians 11:1 (NLT), Paul says, "Imitate me, just as I imitate Christ." We serve as a great resource for families when we have leaders in our ministries who serve as examples for their preteens to imitate. Part of our strategy for Intentional Preteen Ministry is having high school students and young adults who lead in our preteen ministry, in addition to parents. This is one beautiful thing the Church can give a young person: living pictures that show them what they could be like in five years from now, ten years from now, twenty years from now, and beyond. By having consistent volunteers who imitate Christ, we provide an important resource for preteens. They don't have to imitate some random adult movie star. We give them real and accessible people to imitate.

I can still remember one of our kids who changed his hairdo and fashion to match a high school leader in our ministry whom he admired. When you share this truth with your other adult and high school leaders, they start to realize they can have a positive influence. In the book *Sticky Faith*, Kara E. Powell and Chap Clark discuss the idea of a five-to-one goal. We think of a good ratio in our preteen ministry as one leader for every five kids. Powell and Chap challenge us to flip that ratio on its head. What if we tried to put five leaders in the life of every preteen in our ministry? We would have five leaders the preteen could look up to and emulate!

The fact that preteens imitate the adults they admire as they step into identity formation is one of the reasons we play Christian music before and after service. Many preteens are looking for artists and famous people they can emulate. We choose to put Christian examples in front of our preteens. We give them "non-parent adults" whom they can look up to and imitate as they learn how to imitate Christ.

WAY 3: CONFUSING COMPETENCE AND IDENTITY

Erik Erikson studied psychosocial development stages and came to the widely-accepted conclusion that nine-to-twelve-year-old kids are in what he calls "The Competence Stage." This is the stage of life in which they are resolving the issue of industry versus inferiority. They are figuring out, "What am I good at? What am I able to accomplish?" Preteens, according to Erikson, haven't yet arrived at the fidelity stage, which is when they resolve the issue of identity versus role confusion, and ask, "Who am I?"

With preteens, identity is a new issue on the horizon. It starts to emerge as an important issue toward the end of the preteen years. As you work with older, more mature preteens, you'll probably notice that many of them have one foot in the "industry vs. inferiority" stage ("What am I good at?") and their other foot in the "identity vs. role confusion" stage ("Who am I?"). Older preteens have spent a few years working out the answer to the question, "What am I good at?" It's only natural that, as they try to answer the next big question, "Who am I?", they'd be prone to finding their answer in the things they've discovered they are good at.

As a result, some preteens start to confuse their "who" with their "do."

For example, a preteen boy who is highly competent at a certain sport thinks that being an athlete is his identity. He's confusing his "who" with his "do." If he suddenly breaks a leg and isn't able to play that sport anymore, it can be very confusing for him. There are plenty of preteens who confuse competence and identity. We can help.

How do we partner with this approach? One of my responsibilities as I lead preteens is to remember that their desire to be competent is still super important. However, I must also remember to help them separate competence and identity. Our identity as Christians is about who we are as children of God, not what we do. A God-given identity is ours apart from what we accomplish. There's a place for us at His table, and that spot is reserved for us apart from our competence. Even our salvation isn't ours through works.

Jesus was insulted because of who He spent time with. He ate with sinners and tax collectors. But Jesus looks beyond the "do" to the "who." He sees our true identities separate from our abilities and actions. As we emphasize this to preteens and help them to understand the Gospel, we can simultaneously help them understand that God has created them with an identity that is separate from their competence.

WAY 4: LISTENING TO OTHERS

In order to understand who they are, preteens will sometimes listen to what parents or peers say.

Here's what the AMLE says about this: "Young adolescents have a strong need to belong to a group, with peer approval becoming more important, and adult approval decreasing in importance." In other words, preteens are starting to rely on other's opinions of them, and they may start to define themselves by what other people say about them—especially their peers.

How do we partner with this approach? One thing we can do is help preteens understand the limited perspective that humans have. There are so many Bible stories that point to this truth—stories where people's perceptions are totally incorrect:

- The way the Pharisees saw Jesus.
- The way people in Noah's time saw Noah.
- The way David was perceived by Saul.

The list goes on and on and on. It's helpful for preteens when we make that point from time to time using these stories. We can ask, "What did the people think of Shadrach, Meshach, and Abednego? Was that really the truth about them?"

When my younger daughter was ten or eleven, she saw the V.I.P. section at an event we attended and asked, "What does V.I.P. stand for?"

I said, "Very Important Person."

She said, "What? There's no such thing. Except Jesus."

Good answer, Savannah.

That has continued to be her perspective. Even in eighth grade, other people's opinions don't rattle her as much as I've seen them rattle other middle school kids.

Ask most preteens, "How was your day?" and, many times, their answers will be based on what other people said and did. An Intentional Preteen Ministry can help them with this. I feel a responsibility to help preteens understand how limited people's perspectives of them truly are. On the other hand, I want them to see that God's perspective of them is perfect and unlimited.

Many have pointed out that holding up the Bible can be like holding up a mirror, because God sees us clearly. By looking at what He says, we see ourselves. One name for God is El Roi: "The God who sees." El Roi sees you on your good days. He sees you on your bad days. He saw you before you were born, and He sees the last day of your life. Even right now, He sees it all, and He clearly sees who He made you to be.

Let's help preteens learn to look at what El Roi says about who they are instead of being so concerned with what their peers think. Pause for a moment and imagine a banner that could hang above your ministry. There's a statement written on this banner that helps the preteens in your ministry identify who they are. It's a banner that hangs over everything they do and communicates, over and over, to them who they are. What's written on the banner could be something you often teach; maybe it's a go-to verse that you'd really love to help your preteens internalize.

It may be something like the following:

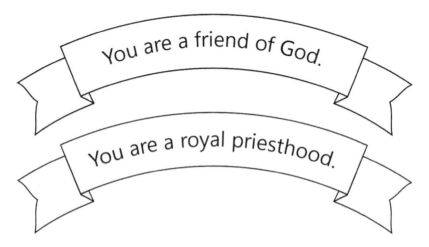

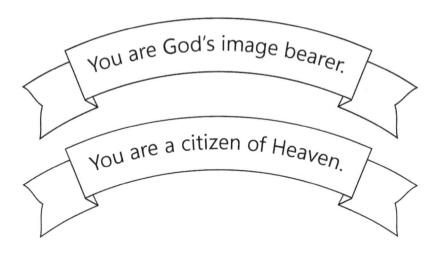

When we literally or figuratively place a banner above our preteens before they've stepped fully into the identity formation stage of development, we're giving them a rock-solid foundation on which to build their identity in the coming years. Let's give our preteens a go-to statement that they can own for themselves when they aren't quite sure about who they are.

IDENTITY FORMATION BECOMES AN ISSUE OF GREATER IMPORTANCE AS PRETEENS MOVE TOWARD THE TEEN YEARS.

We have an incredible, once-in-a-life-time opportunity as we minister to pre-teens: an opportunity to give them the tools to build a rock-solid foundation for their identity instead of being swayed by whatever they feel or by whatever the world says.

What can you help the preteens in your ministry know about who they are? What identity do you want them to embrace about themselves? Who do you want your preteens to know that they are?

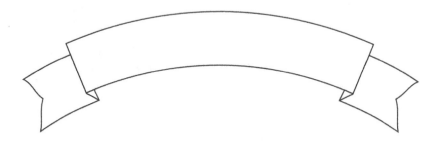

How can you wave this banner over their lives?

ESSENTIAL 9:
PERSEVERE AND OVERCOME OBSTACLES

efore your church gives the green light to a fully-functioning and Intentional Preteen Ministry, there may be questions, objections, misconceptions, or even fears that stand in the way. Raising the value of ministry to preteens in your church is a valuable endeavor, but it's going to be hard work, and your efforts may not be appreciated.

Your efforts may, in fact, be resisted.

One of the greatest indications of whether a church will develop and maintain an Intentional Preteen Ministry is the determination of the ministry leader and his or her team. If there is to be an effective, growing preteen ministry at your church under your leadership, YOUR commitment to its value and implementation is essential. You must have a God-given determination and cry out to Him as the supplier of everything you need in order to stand firm in your desire to help early adolescents step into faith-ownership.

Along the way, you'll likely encounter resistance and challenges. This chapter will encourage you to stand firm by providing two methods for how to lead your ministry as you encounter obstacles.

1. THE GRAND CANYON METHOD

It's amazing that something as "soft" as water can carve incredibly huge canyons into rocks. Often, gentle persistence is the best way forward when facing resistance. A gentle answer can even turn away wrath, according to Proverbs 15:1.

My senior pastor is one of the biggest supporters of our Intentional Preteen Ministry. He talks it in the adult church. He makes sure we're supplied with everything we need to have success. I'm so thankful to God for Pastor Greg and his support; but his attitude about preteen ministry hasn't always been this way.

When I first proposed the idea of a preteen ministry at our church, he said, "I don't think something like that will happen at a church our size." I spent the next two years gently chipping away at his objections:

We started a leadership team for fifth graders. *Chip.*

We started doing Friday and Saturday events for preteens once a month. *Chip.*

We started a special Bible study that met before service for interested preteens. *Chip.*

I brought a group of preteens to Christ In Youth's SuperStart Conference, a weekend event just for preteens. We promoted this in the main church. *Chip.*

I'd comment in staff meetings about how these little things had increased the attendance and engagement of our preteens. *Chip.*

I felt like the persistent widow Jesus talks about in Luke 18:1-8: *Chip. Chip. Chip.*

Two years of this, and the next meeting with my senior pastor went a little differently. When I revisited the idea of a preteen ministry, he asked me to put together a proposal that he would share with the church board. Pastor Greg went from feeling dubious about preteen ministry to being an incredible defender and fan...but it didn't happen overnight. It happened in small, incremental changes in his perception as I chipped away at his objections and slowly painted a picture of what Intentional Preteen Ministry could be.

My experience is not unique. Here's what happened for Eddie at his church in Washington:

> When you see a need that lines up with the passion and calling God has given you, you must act—even if it is a little at time. When I became a volunteer at Christ The King in Burlington, WA, in 2013, I was moved by the excitement and potential the kids had for their faith. While leading a 4th-6th grade Small Group in an elementary setting (K-6th), I started to see a need for them to have their own identity and voice. Several even stopped attending CTK Kids altogether. I saw that preteens (without really knowing that this word even existed) needed a place of their own where they didn't feel they were too old for the group, and where the Small Group discussion was at a different level. They were looking for a place where they could each learn and experience the love of God in a different way than when they were younger.
>
> I had just graduated from college, where I majored in mechanical engineering, but I had a passion for kids to know Jesus, which drove me to educate myself and attempt to become a better leader in the ministry field. During this season, I felt that the most important thing I could do was pray. I prayed that God would be at work in the preteens and strengthen their relationships with Him. My Kid's Ministry Director saw that I was already taking initiative in many areas of

ministry, and serving where there were needs, so she asked me to join the staff on a part-time basis.

I said no, because I worried that, if kid's ministry became a job for me, I would lose passion for the thing that I love. I also experienced a bit of insecurity—I was a young single guy, and honestly, I feared what parents and older volunteers would think of me in a kid's ministry role. As I continued serving in the preteen group every week, I kept praying for them, because I knew they were different than the younger kids in the ministry. Every few months, the Kid's Ministry Director would ask again if I wanted to come on staff. I somehow always knew when it was coming, and had my "No" ready. However, in the summer of 2016, something was different. I knew that the question was coming; but this time, I heard the word "Yes" three times in my spirit. When the Kid's Ministry Director asked me this time, I said "YES."

In the meantime, I continued to grow my understanding of preteen ministry by looking for resources. In early 2017, I found FourFiveSix.org and started to listen to their "Great Ideas for Your Preteen Ministry" podcast and other resources that were mentioned in FourFiveSix.org articles.

This led me to begin intentionally building relationships not only with the kids I ministered to, but also with their parents. While talking to parents, I found myself broadcasting a vision of a ministry geared specifically for these 4th-6th graders. As my vision became increasingly clear, I received resounding support from everyone I shared it with! Raising the value of preteen ministry while casting the vision felt natural. It felt like a must.

During our 4th-6th Small Group times in the elementary setting, I started introducing questions and discussion topics I heard from other preteen leaders. Seeing the levels of interaction among the preteens growing—as did their faith and interest in the Bible—gave me the joy and encouragement to keep on keeping on.

It was at this point that I met Sean Sweet at a Conference in Bellevue, WA. I was able to learn firsthand from him and the FourFiveSix team how to raise the value of my preteen ministry even further. They encouraged me to continue to cast the vision to those around me. I attended online webinars and conferences, as well as the retreat 2 ADVANCE, where I had the opportunity to meet other preteen leaders and see what they were doing. retreat 2 ADVANCE taught me how to be more direct with my vision, and how to develop a vision statement for the ministry!

At this point, I was on fire!

A couple months later, my Kid's Ministry Director asked me to write a ministry proposal. BAM! I had an eleven-page ministry proposal typed in a matter of a few days. I knew what I wanted IGNITE Ministry to be! I was given the green light in August of last year to form the ministry once the leaders came forward. It was time to keep praying for those leaders.

At this point, parents were asking when I was going to start a preteen ministry. My answer was, "Once the leaders come." Within a three-week span, six leaders rose up to the calling, and we were able to do our Ignite Kick Off Event in November of last year, with a Small Group Leader for each gender and grade.

Ignite Ministry has gone through a lot of prayer and effort to become the ministry it is today. It's a midweek youth group for 4th-6th graders. We started it with the intention of meeting one time a month as we slowly moved forward. We've had overwhelming support from leaders, parents, and the kids. We've had so much support, in fact, that last month, we moved to holding this midweek youth group twice a month.

I would not be the leader I am today if it wasn't for all the chipping away. Even though I wanted this ministry to start sooner rather than later, I know that God was preparing me to lead it well, and in just the right timing.

Keep praying for where you are currently and where you want to go. Then, just watch what God does!

I can still remember meeting Eddie at that conference in Washington, and the conversations we had. I can still remember listening as he shared his passion for preteen ministry. It's been such a satisfying experience to watch his preteen ministry take shape, little by little. Eddie, just like the Colorado River, doesn't get offended or depressed at the rocks he encounters. He doesn't give up.

The Colorado River has continued, day and night, to wear away at the rock-hard resistance it faces, until eventually, it has created a mile-wide canyon deeper than the height of THREE Empire State Buildings. Wow!

The Grand Canyon Method says this: persevere as you work on raising the value of your preteen ministry. Keeping Galatians 6:9 in mind can help: "Let us not become weary in doing good, for at the proper time we will reap a harvest if we do not give up."

Chip.

2. THE COMEBACK METHOD

The Comeback Method is something many of us learned when we were preteens ourselves. Back then, it was helpful to have a "comeback" for any possible insult that might be hurled at you. A lot of the comebacks in my circle of friends started with, "Oh yeah? Well..."

Hopefully, we sound a little more mature than we did in sixth grade, but the concept is the same: to have a smart answer prepared for the objections and insults that we may encounter as we develop Intentional Preteen Ministries.

What follows is a list of objections, questions, and fears that people raise when we want to move our preteen ministry forward. Each is followed by what you might use as a "comeback" if you were to encounter them. You can use these to press forward toward Intentional Preteen Ministry—even if some of these objections are coming from within your own head.

Objection: I don't have enough preteens to start a ministry just for them.

Comeback:

If you keep them with the younger kids, that probably isn't going to change.

Here's what I've heard OVER and OVER from people who decided to start a specific ministry to preteens:

"The numbers increased significantly within the first few weeks!"

Usually, the numbers double. Right now, I'm thinking of a weight loss commercial, where the disclaimer at the bottom flashes, "RESULTS NOT TYPICAL." However, when it comes to seeing significant growth in the weeks and months after starting a separate preteen ministry, it's the opposite. The results ARE typical based on all the stories I've heard.

How many preteens do you need to start intentionally ministering to them? Just one.

Sure, it's not going to look the same as a ministry designed with a hundred preteens in mind, but that's beside the point. A ministry to forty preteens is also going to require a different approach than a ministry to 100 preteens.

When you have fewer kids, you have the opportunity to minister in more specific ways. You can plan events around their schedules and get everybody's input about the direction and content they'd like to see in lessons.

I don't want to be the one who buries in the ground what God has entrusted to me simply because it seems like it's not much. I want to be the one who hears, "Well done, good and faithful servant! You have been faithful with a few things; I will put you in charge of many things. Come and share your master's happiness!" (Matthew 25:21, NIV).

Objection: We don't need a preteen ministry; we have them in serving positions in our Children's Ministry.

Comeback:

Just because you're called to Children's Ministry doesn't mean that every preteen in your church is. Although it can be a great first step toward having an Intentional Preteen Ministry, a church isn't done developing an Intentional Preteen Ministry just because they've started a leadership and serving program for preteens to participate in. There is so much more to ministering to preteens.

Imagine if, during midweek services at your church, there was a Men's Bible study, and any women who showed up to church were assigned to serve in it. "That's the extent of our women's ministry here. Isn't that enough?" Would that be the best we could do for women? NO!

We've seen great responses from preteens when they're given opportunities to serve in Children's Ministry, but there is so much more for us to do. What we're communicating to preteens when we have them serve in our Children's Ministry is positive: "We believe you are capable of doing more now that you're older" or, "You aren't too young to be useful in building God's Kingdom." These are great things for preteens to internalize, but there's more they need to learn if they're going to be fully engaged in a lasting personal relationship with Jesus Christ.

Imagine if your whole spiritual journey was whittled down to serving others: no spiritual discussions with peers about topics that you're currently facing; no teaching on how to grow in your own relationship with God; no training on how to sit at the feet of Jesus and simply BE; no one ministering to you; just you ministering to others. This would be an incomplete discipleship program.

Can engaging preteens in serving within Children's Ministry be a positive move forward? Yes! Is it the most we can do? Maybe at first. But it's not the end of the journey! There is still plenty more you can (and should) do for your preteens.

Objection: We've got a lot on our plate as it is, and not enough [resources, volunteers, etc.] to do a preteen ministry.

Comeback:

Maybe it's time to reread Psalm 50.

If it's important to God, He'll provide what we need AS WE GO. Often, in ministry, the provision comes after we take a step in the direction God is calling us—not before. People with far less resources than us have started a preteen ministry and found that God gave them everything they needed to make it an incredibly impactful one.

Do you wait until all the lights are green between here and your destination before you get into your car? Probably not. That's not how life is lived, and that's not how ministry typically works, either. If it's important to minister to the preteens at your church, take one step forward in that direction and see what happens next. God will meet you on the journey, even as you're waiting at the red lights. Just take a step forward.

I've heard of preteen ministries that meet in people's offices, in hallways, and in people's garages while their caring leaders wait for more resources from the Lord. There are preteen groups that meet at a different time from the youth ministry so they can use the youth ministry space. There's always some solution to the issue of lacking resources.

What is God saying to you in Psalm 50:10 (NIV) when He says, "For every animal of the forest is mine, and the cattle on a thousand hills?" In my experience, God's normal way of blessing the faithful is not through preemptive blessing.

Look at Shadrach, Meshach, and Abednego's words in Daniel 3:17-18 (NIV): "If we are thrown into the blazing furnace, the God we serve is able to deliver us from it, and he will deliver us from Your Majesty's hand. **But even if he does not**, we want you to know, Your Majesty, that we will not serve your gods or worship the image of gold you have set up." These three guys knew what was right and did it. Even if they didn't have a contract from God in writing that said He would deliver them from the blazing furnace, they knew that He could, and they took steps toward the fire.

Having something meaningful for the preteens at your church is worthy of taking a step of faith! If you agree, take a step forward and see what Jehovah Jireh does. Even if you don't have the time, space, or resources right now to do everything you envision, what *can* you do for your preteens right now? Do the best you can with what you have, and trust God for the increase. Be faithful (full of faith) with whatever you have now, and I trust that God will give you more.

Stop expecting preemptive blessings. Take a step of faith and see what God does.

Objection: [Parents, pastors, volunteers, etc.] are not on board with the idea of a separate ministry. They don't think it's all that critical to have something separate for preteens.

Comeback:

They don't know preteens, then.

Preteens are distinct from younger and older kids. If we want preteens to take ownership of their faith, we must acknowledge that they are in a unique and critical stage of development that requires a different approach than both younger and older kids.

If it's beneficial to have a separate ministry for any sector of the church, then preteens must certainly be considered. Read the research from Barna Group on this age demographic. Read the AMLE's "Developmental Characteristics of Early Adolescence." Read all the literature on this age group. And share this information with parents, pastors, and volunteers.

- Are preteens unique enough to justify a separate ministry?
- Are they at a precarious point in their development?
- Have other churches seen great fruit come out of starting and maintaining an Intentional Preteen Ministry?
- Are there things that years and years of research have concluded are happening ONLY for nine-to-twelve-year old children?

The answer to all these questions is a resounding

YES.

Preteens are in a unique stage of development, and unless we intentionally create something for this unique stage, we're going to miss out. Preteens are as different from younger and older kids as a butterfly is from a fish. Imagine a butterfly in a habitat designed for fish. This is how preteens feel when we don't build programs designed specifically for them.

To be engaged, they need to be taught in specific ways. Their environment needs to be structured differently if it's going to be optimal for their discipleship needs. Preteens ARE different; they have unique needs that require an intentional approach if we are going to truly minister to them.

Objection: We're just going to group them based on what our local school district does (5th-8th or K-6th, for example).

Comeback:

Why does it matter what grades are in what schools? Kids go to school with students of different grades, sure; but unless they're in a one-room schoolhouse, they typically aren't in a self-contained classroom with kids in different grades.

K-6th graders all going to the same school should be viewed like K-6th graders all going to the same church. Once they enter school, they get split into classes based on grade level (at least for some subjects). We can do the same thing at church and split up the K-6th graders. Typically, K-6th grade schools will even split up recesses, lunches, or assemblies (with K-3rd and 4th-6th having different lunches, for example). A school may include grades K-6th, but they usually aren't bunching all these kids together. The Church can learn from this.

If you're concerned about putting fifth and sixth graders together in a ministry because your school district has fifth grade in elementary school and sixth grade in middle school, remember that most sixth graders don't have any expectation that what happens at school will be mirrored at church. In most situations, it doesn't really matter to many sixth graders. In fact, many of them welcome the opportunity to NOT be the youngest at school AND at church simultaneously.

Many middle school pastors who have 6th-8th grade all together sense that sixth graders are different. This is a critical year. These kids are at an awkward and precarious time in their lives. The only story we have of Jesus from the time He was a baby until He was an adult was of Jesus at age twelve—the same age as most sixth graders.

We added sixth graders into our preteen ministry a few years ago, even though 6th-8th graders are at separate schools from K-5th in many of our local school districts. The sixth graders haven't raised any complaints. They've emerged as leaders in our preteen ministry. It's almost as if they feel the difference between being the youngest and newest at their school and, at church, being the leaders—an opportunity that they seize.

Objection: If we separate fifth or sixth graders from seventh and eighth graders, they'll feel like they're missing out.

Comeback:

The eighth graders probably won't feel that way.

Ten-to-fifteen-year-olds are changing more rapidly than they will at ANY OTHER TIME of their lives, with the exception of zero to two years old. That indicates that putting a fifth grader and an eighth grader together would mean having more of a difference in development than putting a 4-year-old and a 7-year-old together. WOW! Let's think about that again:

> Putting a fifth grader and an eighth grader together means having more of a difference in development than putting a 4-year-old and a 7-year-old together.

Many fifth and sixth graders may initially feel like they're missing out if you separate them from the older kids; but should that be the basis for your decision? A preteen may also feel like he's missing out if he can't take off his seatbelt, stick his entire upper body out the window on the freeway, and scream like a banshee. He may feel like he's missing out if he can't go to a party where there's illegal or dangerous activity. She may feel like she's missing out if she's the only one who has to wear glasses.

Feeling like you're missing out is a normal part of growing up, but it shouldn't be the basis for our decisions as ministry leaders. Instead, we should think about what's best, developmentally, for the preteens in our care. I'm going to repeat something one more time, because I think it's mind-blowing when we consider what it means:

> Putting a fifth grader and an eighth grader together means having more of a difference in development than putting a 4-year-old and a 7-year-old together.

Objection: If we do special things for the older elementary kids, then we must do special things for the younger elementary kids, too.

Comeback:

By separating the preteens out, you WILL BE doing something special for the younger elementary kids!

To NOT lose the attention of older kids, ministry leaders will sometimes skip doing things that would really minister to younger kids. For this reason, younger kids have specific needs that sometimes go unmet when they're in a ministry space with preteens. Wouldn't it be nice to do a silly puppet show or skit, which would be SO engaging to the second graders, and not look up to see fifth graders crossing their arms and rolling their eyes in the back row?

The example that older kids set for younger kids in a mixed age group is not always a positive one. Younger kids will forgo their age-appropriate concerns and behaviors to try to win the approval of the older kids, or to follow the older kids' examples. Splitting off preteens from the younger kids can benefit the preteens AND the younger kids at the same time.

When we first started doing events for preteens, I received a complaint from a long-time volunteer who had a huge heart for younger elementary kids. "Why aren't you doing events for the younger kids, too?"

What I wish I knew to say to her was this: Preteens are different, and different things minister to them. For a preteen, having an event outside of regular service times can be an opportunity to take a step of faith owner-ship. Events give preteens a chance to decide to be a part of the Church—and not simply because it's a Sunday morning or Wednesday night, or because their parents are bringing them. Events give preteens something that they're choosing to do, which helps move them toward faith ownership. Events don't work this way for younger kids. Events for younger kids are, for all intents and purposes, "Family Events."

If you have a heart for preteen ministry and you're concerned that putting attention toward the older kids may raise a few eyebrows, you might be right. However, you can pray that developing better things for preteens will encourage people who are passionate about younger kids to step forward and provide new and better things for the younger kids at your church.

There is one more advantage for the younger kids when you do special things for the older kids: they have something to look forward to. This is an important part of childhood. When the older kids go on trips just for them, have events just for them, and have a leadership program just for them, this creates anticipation and excitement for the younger kids. It gives them a reason to be EXCITED about becoming preteens in your ministry. This is much better than the alternative—younger kids looking at the older kids and thinking, "She looks bored. I wonder if I'll feel that way when I'm a fifth grader, too."

Objection: If I aim at speaking to the older elementary kids, won't the younger kids just fall in line?

Comeback:

When I first started in ministry, I had 1st-5th grade in one room. The advice I received was, "Just aim for the fifth-grade boys." If we're talking about entertainment, this is a great approach. I can tell a joke or a story with this advice in mind and get by. But if I'm talking about intentional discipleship, this approach simply doesn't work. If I'm aiming for the fifth-grade boys, I'll be asking them questions a first grader simply can't understand or begin to answer. I'll be challenging them with things in their spiritual walk that will make no sense to a second grader.

As I look at the topics and methods we use in our preteen ministry, I realize that they would absolutely fail if introduced to the younger elementary kids. When it comes to intentionally discipling kids, preteens are in a completely different world than younger elementary kids. The "aim for the older kids and the younger kids will be fine" approach is not adequate—not if our goal is to minister to spiritual needs in a developmentally-appropriate fashion.

Objection: This is going to be difficult and messy. Isn't it easier to just leave things the way they are?

Comeback:

Buckle up, little camper.

You're a Christian, called to ministry. Since when does this mean that we look for the easy road? Since when is ministry about doing what's expedient instead of doing what's best?

Will it be difficult and messy to make progress on an Intentional Preteen Ministry? Probably so. Will it be worth it? Eternally so.

YOUR COMMITMENT TO A THRIVING PRETEEN MINISTRY WON'T COME WITHOUT RESISTANCE AND CHALLENGE.

That's why an essential part of Intentional Preteen Ministry is a leader who perseveres and overcomes obstacles.

The challenge of ministering intentionally to preteens is a big one, but with the help of the Holy Spirit, you will rise to the occasion. Just take one day at a time. Take one step forward each day, each week, each month. You don't need to be overwhelmed by the size of the challenge. Just persist gently. Soon, you'll sense in your spirit a chipping sound; the same chipping sound that leads to something as vast and majestic as the Grand Canyon.

CHIP.

ESSENTIAL 10:
TAKE THE NEXT STEP

This book has introduced nine essentials of an Intentional Preteen Ministry. However, there's one more that is crucial to success:

Discover your directional goal and take your next step.

This is essential, whether your preteens are currently in a ministry program with other ages or in a ministry that's age-specific.

I use the term *directional* goal to distinguish it from a SMART goal.

Peter Drucker helped to make the idea of SMART goals popular. These goals are:

- **S**pecific
- **M**easurable
- **A**chievable
- **R**elevant
- **T**ime-bound

SMART goals aim at reaching a clearly-defined destination, whereas the types of goals God often lays before us are not about arrival as much as they are about the journey. A God-sized goal isn't about reaching a destination as much as it is about moving in a specific direction.

Think about these God-given goals, and see if you think they fall into any of the same categories as SMART goals:

- "Go into all the world and preach the gospel to all creation." (Mark 16:15, NIV)
- "Be holy because I, the LORD your God, am holy." (Leviticus 19:2, NIV)
- "Work out your salvation with fear and trembling." (Philippians 2:12, NIV)

The point of each of these is movement *in a direction*. The point is not a Specific, Measurable, Achievable, Relevant, or Time-bound destination.

God's calling in my life has always been about direction, not destination. In ministry, I don't wait to experience success when I "arrive" at some SMART destination. I experience success with each step in the direction of my God-given ministry goal.

FINDING ANOTHER STEP TO TAKE IN PRETEEN MINISTRY IS EASY.

You could...

- Plan a preteen-specific event
- Start a Small Group study for preteens
- Start a preteen leadership and service program
- Develop your worship team
- Plan a training for your volunteer leadership team
- Implement an Intentional Preteen Curriculum (or write your own)

I've seen each of these, and many other steps, help different preteen ministries to move forward.

HOWEVER, the first step isn't finding something that attracts your attention like a glittery gem. The first step is developing a clearly-defined and easily-communicated purpose statement. That glittery gem of an idea may be attractive, but it may not be the idea YOUR ministry needs. It may not be a step in the right direction for the Intentional Preteen Ministry that God is calling *you* to lead.

WHAT IS GOD'S DIRECTIONAL GOAL FOR YOUR INTENTIONAL PRETEEN MINISTRY?

I don't have a clue. Without knowing you individually and taking time to hear your heart, I can't even begin to guess. It probably has something to do with Jesus and preteens, but the rest of the details are worth knowing, too.

Each year at FourFiveSix's retreat 2 ADVANCE, ministry leaders discover how to communicate a clear vision of their specific preteen ministry's directional goals. On the last day of retreat 2 ADVANCE, leaders stand up one by one and declare the driving purpose of their preteen ministries. I sit in the back of the room at this annual ceremony, holding back the tears every year. It's an amazing thing to behold. It demonstrates the beautiful truth of God's individualized calling in the lives of His people.

Even though dozens of ministry leaders have gone through the retreat 2 ADVANCE process, I've yet to see two leaders with an identical calling. The amazing Heather Dunn developed the process for retreat 2 ADVANCE many years back, after reading Patrick Lencioni's book, *The Advantage*. Before Heather introduced me to this process, I often fell into the trap of thinking that I needed to copy another church's ministry model or strategies. Sometimes, we leaders try to figure out our ministry's identity by imitating other ministries. This can become counterproductive when we take steps that are not in the same direction as the calling God has specifically given to us.

The fact that something works amazingly for another preteen ministry leader doesn't mean it's going to be right for you. You may have a completely different directional goal than they do. You don't need to have a Fall Festival every year just because the church down the street does one every year with great success. You don't have to start having a VBS just because you saw a church in some Facebook group that runs an amazing VBS with hundreds of preteens. Copying what other churches are doing simply because it's successful for them may actually cause you to move your ministry in the *wrong* direction if the strategy you're copying doesn't line up with your own ministry's directional goals.

All Intentional Preteen Ministries have leaders who are letting go of the bike and running beside, but the purpose with which these leaders do those things varies greatly. God has placed a unique call on each of us. Let me emphasize this final essential again:

Discover your directional goal and take your next step.

Often, we want to skip straight to taking our next step without having a clearly-defined goal. However, having a crystal-clear ministry goal is critical if we don't want to find ourselves taking steps in the wrong direction. To know your next step, you need to know the direction in which you're called to go. Before you begin or change anything in your ministry, take the time to clearly define your directional goal. Write it down. Pray about it. Change it. Pray some more. Rewrite it again. Ask trusted leaders to take a critical look at it with you. Is the goal clear? Is it true? Is it motivating? Is it Spirit-filled?

All the strategies in this book are helpful for the development of an Intentional Preteen Ministry. However, you need to know the specific directional goal of *your* ministry in order to know how to implement these essential strategies.

PUT THE HORSE BEFORE THE CART.

Once you spend dedicated time praying and writing and talking with others to make sure you have a clearly stated directional goal, THEN you'll be able to look at a list of events, curriculum approaches, volunteer strategies, etc. and identify the ones that will move your ministry in the right direction.

You'll also be able to use your directional goal to filter out the approaches that aren't right for your ministry—as fun as they sound and as glittery as they appear. You can find HUNDREDS of free ideas from a variety of ministry leaders at *FourFiveSix.org*. Open this treasure trove of "next-step" ideas that you can use in your preteen ministry: ideas for helping preteens memorize Scripture; ideas for day camps and overnight camps; ideas for missions trips you can do with preteens; ideas for...you name it! But first, have a clear goal, or you may become lost in the glittery gems.

YOUR INTENTIONAL PRETEEN MINISTRY WILL PROBABLY LOOK DIFFERENT THAN EVERYBODY ELSE'S—AND THAT'S GREAT!

Developing an effective preteen ministry is not a cookie-cutter process. I've visited a dozen different ministries in action, and they each had their own unique way of letting go and running beside preteens.

It starts with understanding who your preteens are and what God's directional goals are for you and the ministry you lead. Only then is it effective to look at the resources you have and figure out how to develop a team that uses those resources to move in the direction of your God-given goal. As you develop an Intentional Preteen Ministry, you're not alone. At FourFiveSix, you'll find a community of leaders who are committed to walking beside you as you figure out how to raise the value of your ministry.

To help you take your next step:

- We have peer groups you can join, where you'll find support, training, and ideas in a small group of leaders who get to know one another over the course of 3-6 months.
- We have resources—like a fully-developed curriculum—that embody the strategies explained in this book.
- We have mentoring from preteen ministry leaders—some with more than twenty years' experience working with preteens.
- We have conferences where the Intentional Preteen Ministry community gathers to help support one another.
- We have hundreds of ideas to spark your creativity and give you inspiration for what's next.
- We have trainings to help equip you to figure out your next step.

FourFiveSix, like this book, was not created to give you a one-size-fits-all, step-by-step path toward the development of an Intentional Preteen Ministry; but we'll be there, available to help as YOU figure out YOUR God-given directional goal and YOUR God-ordained next steps. We are there beside you to help, but this ministry is YOURS to figure out. You're going to do great. If things get a little wobbly, you can always email me at *email@fourfivesix.org* or ask a question in the 456 community Facebook group.

Especially as you begin, you may feel like the process of developing an Intentional Preteen Ministry is kind of like...well, learning to ride a bike. You're ready to do things you've never done before, and the results are going to take you to new, exciting places.

The end of the book is here now, friends. The ministry God is calling you to is yours to figure out. Enjoy the ride. As the author of this book, it's time for me to:

Let go...and run beside.